Sell Y Home and Save Thousands on the Commission

Sell Your Home and Save Thousands on the Commission

ROBERT IRWIN

WILEY

John Wiley & Sons, Inc.

Published by John Wiley & Sons, Inc., Hoboken, New Jersey.
Published simultaneously in Canada.

For general information on our other products and services please contact our
Customer Care Department within the United States at (800) 762-2974, outside
the United States at (317) 572-3993 or fax (317) 572-4002.

Wiley also publishes its books in a variety of electronic formats. Some content
that appears in print may not be available in electronic books. For more
information about Wiley products, visit our web site at www.wiley.com.

Library of Congress Cataloging-in-Publication Data:

Irwin, Robert, 1941–
    Sell your home and save thousands on the commission / Robert Irwin.
      p. cm.
    Includes index.
    ISBN 0-471-54851-0 (pbk. : alk. paper)
      1. House selling—United States.   I. Title.
  HD259.I79 2004
  643'.12'0973—dc22

                                                    2003068781

Printed in the United States of America.

10 9 8 7 6 5 4 3 2 1

For Reet, after all these years, still in love.

Contents

Preface

The world is splitting into two camps when it comes to real estate commissions.

Whenever I talk with sellers about listing their property, they complain, sometimes bitterly, about agents' high commission rates: "My house sold for $300,000 and I had to pay the agent $18,000. $18,000! That's serious money . . . and it only took a week to sell!"

On the other hand, when I talk with real estate salespeople, they emphasize their low and sometimes falling income. "With what I have to split with the other broker and my broker and the franchise company, there's less and less for me. If I don't increase commissions, I'll have to get out of the business!" (Some brokers have even started adding a separate transaction fee onto the commission when selling a property to increase their income.)

How is this possible?

Why do sellers feel they are paying too much in commissions, while agents believe they are being paid too little?

Savvy sellers point out that property prices in most areas of the country have increased enormously (sometimes doubling or tripling) in just the past decade. A house that sold for $100,000 a few years ago now may be listed at $150,000, $200,000, or even $300,000.

Yet, although houses are becoming more expensive, the 6 percent commission is still common in most areas. Agents who made $6,000 selling a house a few years ago now may collect a commission of $9,000 to $18,000 on that same house because of price increases.

That's miles ahead of inflation. It's also miles ahead of any additional services that agents may be offering. Because more homes have been resold (on an annual basis) in the United States in the past few years than at almost any other time in history, many sellers think that agents must be getting fat on huge commissions.

Statistics, however, suggest that although a few agents are making big bucks, the average agent earns less than $35,000 a year. Strong competition is a factor—too many agents are struggling to sell a tight inventory of homes. Another problem is that skyrocketing liability insurance has increased the costs of doing business.

Although definitive answers are elusive, the present commission structure no longer seems to make sense. Paying a percentage of the sales price of a listing has been the tradition forever, but it may also be a tradition whose time has run out. It is time to reexamine the fee structure and to consider other ways of paying agents that will stabilize and improve their income while also reducing costs to sellers.

The purpose of this book is to suggest alternatives to the conventional sales commission. Brokers in the field are already implementing some of the methods described in the following chapters. Other ideas are hypothetical—your agent may look at you as if you're from Mars if you suggest them. Nevertheless, all are possibilities worth consideration.

We seek a fair common ground for all parties in real estate transactions by providing a better and steadier income for agents while allowing sellers to save thousands on the sales commission.

Acknowledgments

Special thanks to the many agents who provided guidance for this book and especially my good friends, Beryl and Beau, for the helpful insights they've provided on real estate over the years. Also a grateful acknowledgment to Jason Benjamin for his work in providing research and editing help on the original manuscript.

Sell Your Home and Save Thousands on the Commission

Are You Paying Too High a Commission When You Sell Your Home?

D o you know what is the average commission that home sellers pay to brokers in the United States? Is it 5 percent, 6 percent, 7 percent, or higher?

If you're thinking of selling your home, chances are you said 6 percent. Most people I've talked to believe that although some agents may get 7 percent and a few may get 5, the standard is around 6 percent.

But, is it really so?

Finding out the average commission paid is a tough job. National trade organizations either don't keep records or won't release them probably for fear of being accused of price-fixing. Some national chains may have a flexible commission rate with a bottom figure below which they prefer not to accept a listing, but they are unlikely to reveal this policy. And most data-gathering companies simply don't have this information available.

I was able to find one source: REAL Trends, an online newsletter service that polls 500 real estate companies—both large established chains and what it refers to as the "up and comers." The results are surprising.

According to REAL Trends, the average commission paid in 2002 (the last year the study was conducted) across the United States was 5.12 percent. That represents a 0.25 percent decline from 2001 when the rate was 5.4 percent.

It is important to study that statistic—the average rate of commission paid in the United States was not 6 percent as most people suppose, but instead was only about 5 percent. There was a further breakdown by area of the country:

Area*	Percentage
NE	5.20
MA	4.78

Area*	Percentage
SE	5.50
MW	5.62
SW/MTN	5.16
FW	4.92

* NE: New England: Maine, Vermont, New Hampshire, Massachusetts, Connecticut, Rhode Island, MA: Mid-Atlantic: New York, New Jersey, Delaware, Pennsylvania, West Virginia, Maryland, Virginia, Washington, D.C.; SE: Southeast: North Carolina, South Carolina, Georgia, Alabama, Florida, Tennessee, Kentucky, Louisiana, Mississippi; MW: Midwest: Ohio, Indiana, Illinois, Michigan, Wisconsin, Minnesota, Iowa, Missouri, Arkansas, North Dakota, South Dakota, Nebraska, Kansas, Oklahoma; SW/MTN: Southwest/Mountain: Texas, Montana, Idaho, Wyoming, Colorado, Utah, Nevada, New Mexico, Arizona; FW: Far West: Alaska, Washington, Oregon, California, Hawaii.
Source: Reprinted by permission, Real Trends, Inc., April 2003 (www.realtrends.com).

These percentages suggest that if you live in the Mid-Atlantic states or the Far West (in particular, Washington and Oregon), the average commission rate is below 5 percent.

The preceding data may make you wonder whether, as a seller, you're paying a real estate agent too much to sell your home. After all, if the *average* is around 5 percent and the high, which I've observed, is close to 7 percent, some sellers are paying as little as 4 or even 3 percent in commission. Again, ask yourself, are you paying too much?

Do Agents Earn Their Commission?

What do you get for the money you pay in commission? I have heard sellers say, "I wasted money on my agent. I paid her 6 percent, and within a week three buyers were competing to purchase my home. My agent did nothing to earn her commission!"

Many sellers feel this way because of the big chunk of equity a commission takes out of a home when it sells, particularly in a hot market when homes seem to sell themselves. Most of the time, however, I've observed that agents do work hard for their commission; and in the past, I've always felt that agents were well worth what they got paid. Now, I'm not so sure it's always true.

Consider: If a home sells for $100,000 and the agent receives a 5 percent commission, that's $5,000. On the other hand, if a home sells for $1,000,000 and an agent is paid 5 percent, the commission is $50,000.

Did the agent who sold the million-dollar home do 10 times as much work as the agent who sold the $100,000 home? If not, why is the commission 10 times higher? Or, if the $50,000 commission is justifiable, then is the agent who only got paid $5,000 on the $100,000 home not being paid enough?

Let's look at it from a different perspective. Over the past five years, the prices of homes in most areas have shot up, in some cases doubling. Consider the case of an agent who sold a home for $200,000 five years ago at a 6 percent commission making a total of $12,000 (before splits). Yesterday that same agent sold the same house only now the price has gone up to $400,000. At the same commission rate, 6 percent, the total now paid was $24,000. The commission rate was the same, but the commission cash was double, because of the increase in the price of homes.

Certainly during the past five years the agent's expenses have gone up, especially in errors and omissions (E&O) insurance, but just as certainly, the increase has been nowhere near the amount the price of homes has increased. If this type of increase in cash commissions were in some other industry, for example oil and gas, some in Congress might be screaming "windfall profits!" Perhaps basing the commission on a percentage of the sales price causes the whole problem. Maybe it should be a flat rate instead? Or some combination of minimum flat rate plus a smaller commission?

How Did We Get Here?

Real estate commissions based on a percentage made more sense years ago when home prices weren't so high. In the late 1950s, a small home with basic features might sell for $10,000, and a large home with more amenities might go for $25,000. Back then, most people assumed that the going rate (remember, there actually is no standard rate) of commission was 5 percent (getting 6 percent was unheard of). Thus, the commission on a $10,000 home was only $500. But, the commission on $25,000 home was also only $1,250. The difference between the highest and lowest commission was much smaller, just 2.5 times in our example, because the spread in real estate prices was also much smaller.

As of this writing, the average home in the United States is priced at about $220,000, but million-dollar homes, particularly on the East and West Coasts, are not uncommon. Thus, the price spread is much larger. And so are the commissions.

Thus, we have to ask ourselves, is what worked half a century ago, still appropriate? Is a commission structure based on a simple percentage still justified?

Most agents I know will adamantly insist that it is. They will point out that the typical real estate agent has much more to worry about today than ever before. In the 1950s, home inspections and disclosures were simply unknown. And purchase agreements were typically written on a single page instead of the multiple (sometimes 10 pages and longer) legalistic documents of today. Back then, escrows were easier and closings were far less complex than they are now. And certainly there were far fewer liability issues than there are in our litigious age. And of course, there's the fierce competition between so many agents out there (nearly a million at last count).

All that is certainly true. But, does it justify the commissions that real estate agents receive today? Or are there better ways of dealing with commissions?

New Approaches

In this book, I present a variety of new approaches that some sellers and some agents are beginning to take toward the whole structure of commissions. Indeed, many real estate brokers realize that doing business the old-fashioned way simply won't work anymore. New agents who are creative in their approach to the fee structure for selling a house are changing the landscape of real estate. And while the Internet is not affecting real estate sales as much as originally predicted, it is also slowly eroding the old way of doing business.

The alternatives for paying real estate commissions described in this book are aimed at producing a win-win situation for both the agent and the seller, something everyone can live with.

Following the Money Trail

While you may be fired up about paying a reduced commission when you sell your home, it's also important to be realistic. For example, if your agent is asking for a 6 percent commission and your home is selling for $250,000, the cost to you will be $15,000. So, you may decide to tell your agent that you're willing to pay only half that sum, $7,500, which to you still seems a princely amount.

But, what if the agent's total share of the commission on the sale of your house is only $4,000? And that $4,000 comes out of the half you've chopped off. In essence, you've asked the agent to work for free! Few agents I know, good or bad, will accept that kind of listing.

You may be saying to yourself, "I'm willing to pay $7,500. In what strange way does that mean my agent gets nothing?"

Real estate commission splits can seem strange indeed. Probably the best way to be realistic about negotiating a fair commission with your agent is to understand where the money goes. In the movies (and sometimes in real life), the good guys often follow the money trail. It shows who's getting what and how much. The same thing is true with legitimate businesses including real estate. Following the money is a good way to learn how an agency operates. For most people, the trail ends when they list their home and establish a sales commission. They get their agent, and once the home is sold, they pay their money. End of story.

If you want to become a sophisticated seller, that is only the beginning of the story. You need to understand exactly where that money goes and who gets it. That knowledge will help you determine just how much leverage (or lack of it) you have when negotiating a commission. After all, you can't hope to get a lower commission rate from agents than they receive.

The theme here is that you can't squeeze water from a rock. If you want to negotiate a lower commission rate with your agent, you have to be sure just how big a cut of the commission your agent will realistically get.

Cardinal Rule: The larger the split your salesperson and/or broker get, the more they can discount your commission, if they want to. (Of course, they may refuse any discount at all—we'll see how to negotiate with your agent in later chapters.)

Let's start by following the money trail for some typical commission scenarios.

Sale 1: 6 Percent Commission/50 Percent Agent/Two Realties

This starts off simply enough. We list our house for 6 percent. Our home sells for $250,000. That's bit more than the *median* price for a home nationwide (around $190,000 as of this writing), but it's a good place to begin, assuming the market's rising.

The commission we owe is $15,000. The calculation is easy— you just take 6 percent of $250,000 and you've got it. At the close of escrow, our (the seller's) closing statement shows an expense of $15,000 that goes to the agent's office. (Sometimes the fee is paid directly to the sales agent's office, or it could be split up in escrow between the buyer's agent's office and the seller's agent's office, as will be described shortly.)

We're going to assume that two realty companies, or brokers, handled the sale. This is, by far, the pattern for most sales. Nearly all over the United States, the two realty companies split the commission down the middle (in a few areas there is a 60/40 split with 60 percent to the selling office and 40 percent to the listing office, but we won't consider that variant here). Thus,

XYZ Realty and 123 Realty, each would get half of that $15,000 commission, or $7,500.

It is important to understand that most of the time the specific salesperson we deal with actually works under the auspices of a broker who owns or operates the realty office. Further, most realty offices today are franchises of large national firms. Our salesperson may be Ted, who works for XYZ Realty (broker). Our buyer's salesperson may be Alice, who works for 123 Realty (broker). XYZ and 123 "cobroker" or work together on the sale of our home. At closing, the checks go to the realty companies (brokers). Thus, XYZ gets $7,500 and 123 gets $7,500.

From the raw commission, each company now pays a franchise fee, typically 6 percent. Thus, XYZ's net is $7,050 and 123's net is also $7,050. For convenience, we'll assume the net is $7,000.

Now, each realty company/broker pays the salesperson.

Ted who worked with us, is a "50 percent" salesperson and splits the proceeds from the commission in half with his broker (XYZ Realty). Thus, Ted eventually gets a check for $3,500.

In our first commission scenario, therefore, we pay a total commission of $15,000. However, the salesperson with whom we actually worked directly only gets about 25 percent or $3,500 of $14,000. The rest goes to Ted's broker (realty office) and the buyer's salesperson and her broker. Thus, the basic commission breakdown after payment of the franchise fee is:

Our agent (Ted)	25%	$3,500
Our agent's broker	25	3,500
Buyer's agent (Alice)	25	3,500
Buyer's agent's broker	25	3,500

In this scenario, the agents who did all the heavy lifting (Ted and Alice) only received half of the total commission. The other half went to their brokers, the realty companies. If you're new to the real estate field, this may come as a surprise. You may have thought that the agent who personally worked with you (Ted) should have received a bigger piece of the pie, a larger share of the commission.

In the real world, Ted may have. The 50 percent agents are usually either brand-new agents, or ones who rarely make sales. They receive the lowest cut on the commission scale. As agents gain experience and make more sales, their value increases. In an office with 10 agents, 2 or 3 may make 70 percent of the sales, while the remaining 7 or 8 make only 30 percent.

Agents who are highly productive realize their worth and will come to their broker saying something like, "I'm a top producer. I want and deserve a better break on the commission. If I don't get it, I'll jump to another realty office that will give me a bigger piece of the pie." The broker running the realty has a real problem now. Letting the agent go means losing a top contributor to the office's business. To keep this person, the broker has to offer a better cut. (Note: Some offices are run by a manager with a single broker running a region of offices, however, the effect on commission splits remains the same.)

Thus, most brokerages have a sliding scale of commission rates for their agents. The more productive the agent, the higher the rate. Thus, a better agent may get a 55/45 split; those who are still better, a 60/40 split. For many brokerages, the top rung on the ladder is a 75/25, or even 80/20, split of the commissions the salesperson brings in. (Rarely, a superproducer may make a special arrangement with the broker for more than an 80/20 split, but in that case, the salesperson often must pay for expenses that the broker would normally cover.)

Sale 2: 6 Percent Commission/80 Percent Agent/Two Realties

In this scenario, we are working with the same sales price, $250,000 and the same commission, 6 percent. But while it involves two realties, one representing us and the other representing the buyer, our salesperson gets an 80 percent split; whereas the other salesperson still has a 50 percent split.

———————

Note: The terms "agent," "salesperson," a "broker," "realty office," and "Realtor" all have specific definitions in real estate:

- *Agent.* Anyone licensed to sell real estate whether a broker or a salesperson. All agents must pass usually rigorous testing on the real estate law and business practices in their state.
- *Salesperson.* A licensed agent who must work under the auspices and tutelage of a broker. Typically, a salesperson is a new agent just learning the business. In some states, a salesperson must work a minimum of two years for a broker before applying for a broker's license. Salespersons normally cannot receive a commission from a client (you). Their employer (the broker) is the only one who can pay them.
- *Broker.* A licensed agent who can work independently and is entitled to collect a commission. A broker can hire any number of salespeople.
- *Realty office.* An office established by a broker and usually having several salespeople working in it. The broker

runs the office and is liable for all transactions that occur through it. Also called a brokerage.

- *Realtor.* A broker member of the National Association of Realtors (NAR), a national trade organization representing agents and dedicated to increasing the education and ethics of its members. Salespeople can be Realtor Associate members.

As before in our example, each broker/realty gets half of the total commission. Ted's broker gets $7,000 and Alice's broker gets $7,000 after paying franchise fees. But now, the split between agents is different because Ted is going to get 80 percent of the $7,000 his broker receives:

80 Percent Commission Breakdown

Our agent (Ted)	80%	$5,600
Our agent's broker	20	1,400

On the other hand, Alice gets the same breakdown as before since she's only a 50 percent agent.

50 Percent Commission Breakdown

Buyer's agent (Alice)	50%	$3,500
Buyer's broker	50	3,500

What's important is that if our agent, Ted, is an 80 percent agent, he gets nearly twice as much commission as a 50 percenter. This has important ramifications for us. First, while a 6 percent commission, or $15,000, may seem like a lot of money to us as sellers (because we have to pay it), there might not be a whole lot to play with if we're negotiating a reduced commission.

By the time the brokers split the commission between the listing and selling offices (and the franchise companies) and by the time the salesperson splits with the broker, the pot has diminished significantly. Instead of being able to negotiate a discount on a $15,000 commission, perhaps we can only negotiate it on half of that (after franchise fees), assuming that both broker and salesperson go along. If we are dealing with a 50 percent salesperson, he or she may only stand to be getting a few thousand from the deal.

How realistic is it to ask an agent who is making $3,500 to $5,600 to take a $5,000 cut? It is tantamount to asking the person to work for free, or worse!

The problem comes about because the commission is split so many ways. If it can be split fewer times, then there's more money for us to negotiate over. This happens when the same company that lists our house, also sells it.

Sale 3: 6 Percent Commission/80 Percent Agent/One Realty

Now we'll again assume a $250,000 sales price and a 6 percent commission. And we'll assume our agent, Ted, is still an 80 percenter. Instead of two brokers (two realty offices), however, the same realty produces both the buyer and seller (us). Another XYZ agent, Jean, brings in the buyer.

Now our check goes entirely to XYZ office. After paying the 6 percent franchise fee off the top, the broker then splits with the two agents. Ted, gets a commission for representing the seller; Jean gets a split for representing the buyer.

Typically, the broker first splits the commission in half. The $15,000 (minus franchise fees) now becomes $7,000 and $7,000. Then, the salespeople get their splits:

The One-Office Commission
Split (All to ZYX Realty)

Buyer's half	$7,000 (after franchise fee)
Seller's half	7,000 (after franchise fee)

The Split to Salespeople

Seller's salesperson (Ted: 80%)	$5,600
Broker (XYZ)	1,400
Buyer's salesperson (Jean: 50%)	3,500
Broker (XYZ)	3,500

With only one office but two salespeople involved, the salespeople essentially get the same commission that they would receive if there were two separate brokers/offices. The realty, however, gets much more: 20 percent of the fee for the seller's agent (Ted's fee) and 50 percent of the fee for the buyer's agent (Jean's fee). The broker/office ends up with $4,900.

Note: Not all offices operate like this. In some cases, the broker reduces its cut and increases the salespersons' cuts when a single office is involved.

Dealing with only one office doesn't necessarily increase your leverage for obtaining a lower commission rate with your salesperson. But, it could represent an opportunity simply because the office gets a bigger piece of the pie.

Sale 4: 6 Percent Commission/One Agent/ One Agency

To carry this a step further, What is the commission split if your salesperson both lists *and* sells your home? Now the transaction involves only one salesperson and one broker.

When you pay your $15,000 commission, it goes straight to the broker (roughly $14,000 after the franchise fee). If Ted (your agent) is an 80 percenter, then he gets roughly $11,200. Ted gets both the buyer's and the seller's portion of the commission. (Of course, if Ted is only a 50 percenter, then he only gets $7,000.)

Nevertheless, it's easy to see that the salesperson has much more money on the table to play with. Because the commission is bigger, the seller has more room to negotiate a lower rate directly with Ted. The problem is that normally no one knows who will bring in the buyer until long after the seller and the realty have agreed on the commission and signed the listing:

One Salesperson, One Broker Split

Ted	80%	$11,200
Broker	20	3,800

Sale 5: 6 Percent/Broker Only

We're going to refine this even further. Let's say that instead of going to a large office, you go to a one-person office. Here, there are *no* salespeople. The broker runs her own office and since this is not a franchise, there is no franchise fee to pay. Shirley is an independent, a solid producer; who loves to be free of the rules, policies, and fees associated with a franchise office. She's broker and salesperson all rolled up into one.

Note: A person with a broker's license can work as a salesperson under another broker. Top producers who also happen to be brokers often "park" their license under another broker who is a member of a national franchise. Shirley, however, is a broker who works entirely for herself.

Shirley maintains an office and specializes in selling residential property . . . and she's very good at it. She lists your property and finds a buyer for it. When you write your $15,000 commission check, it all goes right into Shirley's pocket. No splits of any kind are involved unless another realty office happens to produce a buyer.

Because one person controls so much of the commission in this scenario, it is perhaps your best chance to negotiate a smaller rate. The fewer the splits, the fewer the people involved, the more any one agent gets. Of course, we are only talking about the *ability* of an agent to cut the commission. This does not mean that the agent is *willing* to do so. That problem is covered in later chapters.

Sale 6: 4 Percent Commission/50 Percent Agent/Two Agencies

Before looking at the expenses that both a typical agent and a typical office incur, let's consider a slightly different scenario.

Here you have listed your home for a 4 percent commission with a broker who offers discounts (see Chapter 4). You might think that everything proceeds as it did in the earlier examples, except for splitting a smaller commission. But that's not how it works in real life.

In many, perhaps most cases where there's a lower commission, the reduced amount is *borne entirely* by the listing office. The selling office gets a much larger slice of the pie.

For example, with a 4 percent commission, 3 percent (75 percent of the commission) would likely go to the selling office. Only 1 percent (25 percent of the commission) would likely go to the listing office.

Thus, if the commission amount was $10,000 (4 percent of a $250,000 sale), the realty office that found the buyer would get (forgetting franchise fees for the moment) $7,500, whereas the selling office would only get $2,500:

Reduced Office
Commission Split

To selling office	$7,500 (3%)
To listing office	2,500 (1%)

This also means that the listing salesperson and his or her office have a much smaller split. If they split 50/50 they'd each get only $1,250:

Selling Agent/Office Split

To salesperson	$1,250
To office/broker	1,250

With some discount brokers, the salesperson does not get a commission at all, but instead is on a salary.

Why Give the Selling Office the Lion's Share?

Why does the selling office get so much and the listing office so little when the commission is reduced? (The commission can be divided up on a 3/1 basis—1 percent to the listing realty, 3 percent to the selling realty.) It might be divided up 2/2 or even 2.5/1.5. Any division can be made.

The answer is that almost all properties are cobrokered and listed in the Multiple Listing Service (MLS) so other offices and salespeople can work on them. However, as in most other things, the realities of a competitive marketplace are operative. To get a buyer's agent to work on your house, you have to offer a realistic commission.

Look at it from the perspective of the buyer's agent. Is that agent going to be willing to spend whatever time it takes to produce a buyer for your home if you only offer a 1 percent commission? Or is the buyer's agent more likely to spend the time and effort if you're paying a 3 percent commission?

I don't know about you, but if I were an agent searching through a listing book with thousands of properties to find homes to show a buyer, I'd let my finger linger a little longer on listings for a 3 percent commission than for a 1 percent commission. Ethically, I'm supposed to find the best home for my client, the buyer, regardless of the commission rate. But in the real world, there are probably a dozen homes that will do just as well. And if some are listed for 3 percent and others for 1 percent, which would you be inclined to show?

Thus, as a seller, it's to your advantage to give the buyer's agent as large a share of the commission as possible to facilitate a sale. That means the only other place you can cut is the seller's agent's portion. Thus, instead of giving the *listing* agent/broker 3 percent (assuming the full commission would be 6 percent), we might negotiate down to a 1 percent fee.

It is important to remember that we usually get what we pay for. For a reduced fee, we may get reduced assistance in selling our home. This risk is covered in detail in later chapters, but keep in mind that there's no free ride in real estate, or in most other places.

Sale 7: 1 Percent Commission/80 Percent Agent/One Agency

Finally, let's take an extreme case to see why cutting commissions drastically is an unlikely proposition. We list our home for a 1 percent commission. Since it's unlikely that other brokers will actively work on this listing, any buyer will probably come from our own agent/broker. Let's assume that our agent, Ted, does find a buyer. Here's how the commission would break down (again forgetting about franchise fees). The commission to the office would be $2,500. And Ted would get 80 percent of that or $2,250. The office's share would be only $250.

It is easy to see why very few, if any, agents or realty offices will accept a 1 percent fee.

Are There Any High-Income Agents?

The preceding discussion might have given you the impression that being in real estate is a relatively low-paying job. Actually, that's the way it is for many members of the profession. A 50 percent salesperson who receives the typical commission of around $3,500 for selling the average house (see preceding examples) needs to sell at least one house every month and a half or so just to come close to earning $30,000 income annually (which approaches what the average salesperson makes nationally). And selling a house every month and a half or so, while an admirable goal, is not something most agents accomplish. To make a $100,000 annual income, the salesperson would have to sell two and a half houses a month, which is very difficult. But achieving this rate of sales would make the salesperson a top producer entitled to a much higher percentage of the commission.

Agents who sell large amounts of property sometimes do extremely well. In high-value areas where the average home sells for half a million or more, top agents (who, of course, are in the minority) can measure their income well into the mid-six figures. The majority of agents measure their incomes in the mid-five figures.

Is There an Additional Transaction Fee?

When you sign a listing, your salesperson typically will sign it as the broker's representative. (The exception would be a salesperson who is also the broker.)

What should be evident is that most of the sales the office makes go to the top producers who are generally paid 75 to 80 percent of the commission the office receives. As a result, the top salespeople are getting the lion's share of whatever commissions there are to split, and the office is getting the lamb's share.

Yet, maintaining the office involves many routine expenses. Even if the 80 percent agent bears a portion of the listing costs, the office must still pay for a front on a street as well as a receptionist/secretary, furnishings, utilities, and an advertising budget. The problem with so many of the top producers getting 80 percent is that the office share can get whittled down until it does not always cover the overhead. Thus, some large brokers (sometimes members of national chains) have started charging a "transaction fee." It goes by many names, but it's a set fee that the seller (and sometimes the buyer) pays directly to the realty office/broker over and above the commission (which the broker splits with the salesperson).

In selling our $250,000 home, the broker—after negotiating a 6 percent ($15,000) commission—might add a $500 transaction fee. This money bypasses the salesperson (Ted) and goes directly to the broker/realty office. Most sellers, understandably, are outraged when they find a transaction fee squeezed into their listing agreement, their sales agreement, or their escrow instructions. "Why," they may say, "Should I pay an extra $500 on top of the 6 percent or $15,000 that I'm already paying?"

When the broker tries to explain the economics of running a real estate office, the sellers are typically unimpressed. "That's your problem, not mine. You work it out with your salespeople—don't try to get it out of me!"

Quite frankly, I agree. Regardless of the harsh economics of running a real estate office, it should never be the client's obligation to bail out the broker. I would not pay a transaction fee. (Be careful when you sign your listing. If the fee is included and you don't notice it, you could be legally obligated to pay it.)

The Agent's Expenses

The goal here is not to cry over the costs of working in real estate, but to look at the real estate agent's expenses in a more realistic light. That knowledge is useful in determining how big—or how little—a commission cut the seller can reasonably ask for or hope to obtain.

All agents, whether they are 50 percenters or 80 percenters, have certain expenses:

- *Clothing.* Yes, we all have to buy clothes. But to maintain an image of success, those in the real estate business need a higher-end wardrobe for meeting clients.
- *Car.* Again, we all need a car. But in addition to needing a vehicle for convenience in transporting clients, an agent needs to look successful, which usually translates into driving a luxury vehicle. The agent must factor in the cost of gas and maintenance to keep such a car on the road plus the expense of leasing or buying a new car more often.
- *Phone.* Even if the office provides a phone, the agent needs a cell-phone.
- *Insurance.* All agents need to carry "errors and omissions" insurance in case a deal goes bad and a seller or buyer sues. And there's also liability insurance in case a client falls or gets hurt while being shown property. As with all insurance, the costs are getting higher. And although the broker may bear some of the burden, salespeople often must pay part of the premium as well.

In addition, those agents who get a bigger cut of the commission may have to contribute a larger share toward covering the office's overhead. This can include the following expenses:

- Business cards and stationery
- Website
- Office furnishings (desks, file cabinets, carpeting)
- Office equipment (fax machines, computers, copiers)
- Office utilities (phones, DSL line, water, gas, electricity)
- Space (sometimes the agents must rent space from the broker)

These are just a few of the expenses. Agents may have frequent facial treatments and hair appointments so that they look their best all the time (after all, their business involves meeting people). And the agent may need a personal secretary to help with clients and scheduling. And we haven't even mentioned all the evenings and weekends that the agent shows property and works at open houses. Many of these expenses, such as for clothing and a higher priced car, may not even be tax deductible (agents should always check this out with their accountant).

Again, the intent in this chapter is not to lament the difficulties of being a real estate agent in today's marketplace. When attempting to negotiate a lower rate of commission, however, it is essential to understand the agent's perspective. You can then be realistic about what the agent may or may not be able to do—or simply is not willing to do.

The agent's position may be much like the dilemma you, as a seller, would have if a buyer were to ask you to accept less than the amount you owe on your house. No matter how badly you might like to accept the offer, you couldn't do so because you don't have enough equity to play with. (On rare occasions, a seller can get the lender to accept a "short sale," or less than the amount owed—an exception that requires a more technical explanation than can be provided here.)

Similarly, if you ask agents to take a lower commission than the amount they need to make on the deal, they are likewise unable to accept, no matter how much they would like to have your listing. Asking them to cut their commission even slightly may mean they can't cover their expenses in the business. It's something to consider as we move on to the following chapters.

 **3**

Know What
You Want from
Your Agent

Placing an order is easy when you know what you want. If you want a steak, you can pick just the right restaurant to serve you the best New York cut, T-bone, or top sirloin. Decisions about dining out are simple if you know what you want.

The same holds true for most other things in life. If you know that you want a convertible, you're not going to waste time looking for a coupe or a sport-utility van. Want a science fiction book? Then you're unlikely to search for it in the romance, mystery, or action/adventure sections of your bookstore.

The key to *finding* what you want is *knowing* what you want. And that holds true with real estate as well. Most people, however, don't have the slightest notion what services they want their real estate broker to provide, other than "Sell my house!"

Yes, of course, sell your house. But using what techniques? And furnishing what kind of assistance? And being on call to handle what sort of paperwork? If you simply say, "Do what it takes," you're probably going to pay a high price. It's sort of like taking your car into a garage and saying, "Fix it." Don't expect to pay anything less than top dollar. But if you know what you want and can pick and choose from the agent's services, you may be able to achieve significant savings.

Services That Agents Can Provide

It's important to understand that agents don't sell your house. You're the only one who can sell your home, because you're the one who owns it. The agent can offer you various forms and levels of assistance in selling that home (sometimes at a variety of prices). If you know which services you want the agent to provide, you will be in a better position to negotiate the terms of the commission.

I was recently negotiating with a builder for the construction of an addition to a home that I own. I didn't simply tell the builder, "Here's the plan, do the job." Instead, I carefully outlined exactly what I wanted the builder to do. He was to handle all the rough work—foundation, framing, plumbing, electrical work, insulation, and drywall. But, he was *not* to do any of the finish work for the plumbing, wiring, painting, or trim. I would do that. Since the finish work often represents as much as 35 percent of the cost of the construction, I was able to negotiate a much lower price than I would have paid if I had simply given him the plans and said, "Do it!"

In real estate, everything is negotiable including the rate of commission that you pay an agent for selling your home. In Chapter 4, I explain how to negotiate the commission with an agent. Before undertaking that task, however, you need to know exactly what you expect that agent to do for you. If you don't, you may end up paying more than necessary or getting less assistance than you want or need.

When the Standards Are Unclear

In real estate, you're unlikely to find a widely accepted "standard of service." It is more or less up to each agent (salesperson and broker) to do whatever seems appropriate to sell your home, as long as it's legal and ethical. (The National Association of Realtors does offer a "Code of Ethics and Standards of Practice" that is mainly a guide to ethical conduct and on which many state regulations are based.) One agent might rely on extensive advertising. The next agent might do no advertising at all but rely on word-of-mouth.

Because there is no official standard for the way to sell a home, it is difficult for most sellers to know what to expect from their agent. In this chapter, I describe typical services that full-service agents provide. When you talk with your agent, ask whether these services will be available and if not, why not?

Keep in mind that no agent *must* offer all these services. Indeed, almost no agent will *guarantee* to sell your home. (Some will guarantee to buy your home if it doesn't sell, but that's a different book.)

Typical Services of Real Estate Agents

Advertising

Advertising is an essential part (or should be) of every home sales plan. To find the one right buyer for your home, you have to let many potential buyers know it is for sale and what it has to offer. Think of it as a numbers game. If one buyer in a thousand is perfect for your home, on average you have to reach a thousand would-be buyers to get to just that right one. Advertising can do this for you.

For you to advertise your home on your own would be very expensive, particularly for a large ad. (A small FSBO [For Sale by Owner] ad would be more feasible; see Chapter 12.) A real estate agency can offer lots of advertising for your home, both locally and nationally. The office probably lists dozens of homes, and its large ad can feature many of them. Even if your home is only mentioned in a few lines or with a small picture, the ad will catch buyers' attention, bring them in, and allow agents to show them to your home.

Further, assuming that your home is *cobrokered* (your agent allows other agents to work on it), you benefit from the advertising those agents do in the area. Even though the ads don't mention your house specifically, agents can switch buyers who call in about advertised homes, if your home happens to have what they are looking for.

A huge advertising system for buyers is in place and ready to go to work, just waiting for you to tap in. And your agent holds the key to it, if you want it.

Cleaning

Most people understand that to sell their home, they need to clean and fix it up. Real estate agents often talk about "curb appeal," meaning the first impression your home makes on a buyer. You want to make a good first impression and having your home clean and attractive is the way to do it.

At the same time, most sellers are busy doing other things with their lives than cleaning up their homes. While most of us maintain a minimum level of cleanliness, we may have kids to wash, dress, and get off to school; we have demanding jobs and must maintain our work clothes; we prepare meals and do the laundry; and we try to find a little bit of time to relax (a vitally important part of life). Many people simply don't have the time or desire to get their home into that spotless shape buyers love to see.

Some real estate agents can handle this problem for you. Their offices contract with cleaning crews, and as soon as you list, they send a crew out (at the agency's expense) to clean your home. These professional cleaners come in and scrub down the bathrooms, the kitchen, and the floors. They wash the windows, remove marks and spots from the walls, and put your home in first-class shape.

Of course, it's up to you to keep it that way during the showing period until a buyer is found. But it is a lot easier to maintain a clean property than to do the initial cleaning. Not every agent offers this service. But some agents, who are particularly aware of the problems of busy sellers, perform it on a regular basis.

Closing

Most sellers think of closing the deal, the period between the time buyers and sellers sign off on the sales agreement and escrow close/title changes hands, as a formality. The major effort is to find a buyer and get a signed agreement.

Nothing could be further from the truth, especially in today's market. It is during the closing period that the real estate agent often has the most work. This includes providing disclosure statements to you (see following section), getting buyers to remove contingencies, checking to be sure title is clear, following the buyer's progress in obtaining financing, and arranging for the escrow to close.

There's nothing to prevent you or someone else from handling all these chores. But to do so, you need to know what they are, how to prioritize them, how to deal with them, and what the warning signals are. Don't assume that the escrow officer handles all these details. The escrow officer simply receives and prepares documents and handles monies. Escrow officers in today's world normally won't lift a finger to help you get a termite clearance or to provide you with federal disclosure statements. They remain neutral and simply run the escrow.

It is the real estate agent who typically manages the closing for the seller (and the buyer) and sees that everything is ready for a timely closing. Not all agents are as conscientious as they ought to be, and sometimes through carelessness or lack of attention, deals fall apart. Nevertheless, this assistance is usually available, if you desire it.

Disclosing

In today's world of selling real estate, most states require that you provide the buyer with a statement disclosing defects in the property. In some cases, legislation specifies what must go into the disclosure statement. In other states, the law is less precise. In addition, most buyers make their purchase offer contingent on your providing a detailed disclosure.

Finally, as of this writing the federal government requires sellers to give buyers a specific disclosure statement regarding lead in the home and provide a booklet on the hazards of lead poisoning.

You can obtain this information from websites such as www.epa.gov as well as state government sites. Usually, however, a real estate agent can provide you with the forms and all the necessary materials. And, if you're in doubt about something, the agent can help you in filling out the form, and explain what you need to say on it.

Documenting

All sorts of documents are required in a real estate transaction. They begin, usually, with the sales agreement and continue with preliminary and final escrow instructions, abstract of title, deed, and more.

If you have handled many real estate transactions, you are probably well aware of all the required documents. You can either obtain the documentation yourself or get an attorney to provide it for you.

Normally, a real estate agent can handle all the documentation involved in a transaction. The agent not only can provide it, but also can explain the purpose and meaning of each document. (This can be particularly helpful in interpreting such things as an Abstract of Title report.)

Again, the agent is there with the assistance, but only if you want and demand it.

Financing

As a seller, you are unlikely to be directly involved in financing (unless you are purchasing another home or are handling the paperwork for the buyers). Almost always, however, the buyers of your home must obtain financing, and that can cause many problems. Financing difficulties are the number one cause of deals falling through.

Responsible agents check out the buyers' financing very closely. This begins when you receive an offer and your agent checks to see that the buyers are "preapproved." Preapproval means that the buyers have gone to a lender who has checked their credit and income to verify that they can qualify for a needed mortgage.

Note: Preapprovals are worthless unless they include a commitment from a lender to offer financing. Your agent can (or should be able to) check for that commitment.

Once escrow opens, your agent should be calling the buyer's agent (and sometimes even the buyer) at least once a week to check on their progress in obtaining financing. Just because there's been a preapproval doesn't necessarily mean that financing will be forthcoming. A problem with the buyer's income, credit, or cash reserves may turn off a lender. Or the lender itself could be unable to fund the loan.

A critical function of your agent is to track the buyer's financing. If there are problems, your agent should start waving the red flag. As early as possible, the agent should notify you that the buyers are having problems and let you know whether they are minor, serious, or fatal to the financing. That way you can start preparing to put your house back on the market and redirect your efforts to reselling it.

Successful agents give top priority to a buyer's financing.

Hand-Holding

No adult likes to admit the need to hold onto someone's hand, but if you're new to real estate, this may be exactly what you need.

Most of us have heard of *buyer's remorse.* It occurs right after a buyer makes a purchase and starts thinking about having spent all that money. The buyer gets depressed and begins trying to back out of the deal. Sometimes buyer's remorse becomes so intense that it actually ruins a deal.

Something like this happens with sellers, too, right after signing the sales agreement. Seller's remorse hits you when you suddenly fully realize that you've sold the old homestead, that you're actually going to have to move, that the old door frame on which you notched the heights of your children will be sanded clean and painted.

Some sellers want to renege on the sale. Others simply can't function and go forward. An agent who is on hand to smooth the way can help you start thinking ahead about the adventure on which you are embarking—about your new home and a new and presumably better life.

The agent can offer the same helpful assistance when you begin worrying about a defect in the house or a problem with your lender who wants to charge you too much in a payoff, or an escrow officer who seems unreceptive to your concerns.

The agent can hold your hand, help you through these emotional crises, and save the deal.

Holding Open Houses

Most sellers want, indeed demand, that agents hold at least one or more *open houses*. They believe this is one of the best ways to attract buyers and get a quicker sale. The truth is that relatively few buyers buy the home they visit on an open house. Instead, an open house for buyers is the agent's recruiting office for clients. The agent hopes to sign up new buyers and sellers from among those who visit.

What can really be helpful are open houses exclusively for other agents. The idea is to spread the word about your home to others in the field. The more agents are aware of your property, the more likely they are to show it to buyers they have. And the quicker you're likely to sell.

Holding an agent's open house is much like "caravaning," where your agent invites others in his or her office (and other offices as well) to tour your home on a set day. Dozens, sometimes hundreds, of agents may come by to see it. And one of them may just have the right buyer for the property.

Open houses for agents and caravaning are services an agent can offer, especially if you demand them.

Inspections

These days you can automatically expect that the buyers will want a professional home inspection to determine the condition of your home. Often they will write the demand for an inspection right into the purchase agreement as a contingency (the purchase is "subject to" your allowing the inspection). They will typically want 14 days to find an inspector, conduct the inspection, pay for it, and approve it. Your agent should insist that you get a copy of the report.

Your agent can be a big help in determining whether you should have an inspection prior to putting your home on the market. If you suspect problems, you may want to pay for your own inspection to find out their extent. That way you can have repairpeople of your choice correct the problems, before the buyers learn about them. (This is not to say that a repaired problem shouldn't be disclosed—it should be, along with the method of repair.)

Another area where your experienced agent can help is in interpreting the written inspection report and deciding how to answer demands from the buyer for repairs. Does a problem need immediate attention, or is it a minor one that should be overlooked? Your agent may also know repairpeople who are quick, efficient, and charge reasonable rates.

When you're handling the buyer's inspection, your agent can be an invaluable resource.

Listing

Certainly your agent will want to list your property. After all, that's how the agent gets paid. There are several listing options. We discuss the following basic listing options at length in Chapter 9:

- *Exclusive right-to-sell:* Your agent gets paid no matter who sells the property, even if it is you. This is, understandably, the preferred (sometimes the only) option presented by most agents.
- *Exclusive agency:* Your agent gets paid no matter what other agents are involved, but does not get paid if you sell the property entirely on your own. Most agents will not

accept this listing because they fear you'll sell the property out from under them.

- *Open listing:* Here you pay any agent who brings in a buyer. Most agents again will refuse to work hard on this because they fear another agent may make the sale.
- *Net listing:* You set a maximum price. Anything over that price, the agent gets to keep. The problem here is that the agent might end up making a huge commission—money that you may feel is rightfully yours.

All these listing options are available. It is up to you to choose the one you want to pursue.

Preparing the Sales Agreement

The sales agreement is the document that holds the deal together. It expresses the intent of the buyer and seller and details the price, deposit, down payment, financing, contingencies, and more time for closing. The document is intended to be legally binding, so you need to make sure it is completed properly.

It is not mandatory to have an agent handle the sales agreement. You can handle it yourself, or you can have your attorney prepare it. However, since it's so intimately involved in the negotiations over price and terms, it's usually best to have the agent fill it out. Most agents provide their own sales agreement, which is typically many pages long and is filled with boilerplate legalese. They fill it out and are responsible for it.

Promoting

In addition to advertising, there is another kind of promoting that is vitally important, and it is a service that only an agent can perform.

Remember, a huge system is in place to help you sell your property. It comprises all the agents in the surrounding area. They are typically interlocked by the Multiple Listing Service (MLS), which allows them all to work on your listing. However, yours is only one of hundreds, perhaps thousands, of listings. Why should they show your home instead of others?

The reason is that your agent is promoting it to them. We've already mentioned caravans and open houses and offering the listing office a good commission rate. However, there are other means. At meetings that agents regularly attend, your agent can "talk up" your house, "press the flesh" in one-on-one contacts with other agents, and can send e-mails and faxes. And your agent can put your home on a website to obtain additional exposure.

Promoting your home to other agents is a great service an agent can perform, if you want it.

Screening

You don't want just anyone coming in to see your home. There are the wannabe buyers who can't possibly afford your home. There are the future sellers who are sizing up the competition. There are tourists who have nothing better to do than to check out homes for sale. And then there are those who have darker thoughts on their minds such as robbery.

Your agent can screen all the people who want to see your home, keep out most of the unwanted. Although you have the right to view all offers, your agent also can help you go over your offers and understand which are sincere (offer you a good price and a reasonable chance of closing) and which are frivolous (lowballs from potential buyers hoping to steal your property or dubious offers that have little chance of ever closing).

It is very useful assistance, available at your request.

Showing

You can show your home to potential buyers. Or your agent can show it for you. If you think this is an easy task, I suggest you try showing your home to buyers sometime. Unless you're experienced, you won't know how much to say—or how little. You won't know when to apply pressure to buy—and when to lay back.

Worst of all, when the buyers leave, you won't be able to discuss your property with them to determine whether they're serious and are likely to make an offer.

For-sale-by-owner sellers often describe showing their homes as the most frustrating part of the sales process. An agent will be happy to handle it for you, if it's the kind of assistance you want.

Using Signage

Finally, there's the sign in front of your house. It is possibly the most important sales tool since it draws attention to what is for sale. Another good idea is to have a box on the sign with flyers that describe the features of your home and state the price. You can easily get your own sign and stick it in the ground. Or the agent can provide you with it, as you wish.

Agents take care of signage as a matter of course. They have the signs ready although they often pay someone to come out and put the sign in, particularly in areas where zoning ordinances require adherence to signage restrictions.

These are most of the services that agents can perform for you. In negotiating their fee with them, keep in mind how many (all or only a few) of them you want the agent to perform. If you can eliminate some of these services, you might be able to get the agent to charge considerably less.

CHECKLIST
In Which Areas Do You Want
Assistance from an Agent?

[ ] Advertising

[ ] Cleaning

[ ] Closing

[ ] Disclosing

[ ] Documenting

[ ] Financing

[ ] Hand-holding

[ ] Holding Open Houses

[ ] Inspecting

[ ] Listing

[ ] Preparing Sales Agreement

[ ] Promoting

[ ] Screening

[ ] Showing

[ ] Signage

Discount Agents

A revolution in real estate commissions is taking place. By some estimates, as many as 10 percent of all real estate companies now offer discounts up front. You can obtain a discount that ranges between 1 and 2.5 percent simply by walking in the front door (or contacting the company over the Internet).

Nowhere is this more obvious than in the discounts offered by many retailers, credit unions, and corporations. In some areas, shoppers' clubs such as Costco and Wal-Mart have offered discount services for their members through arrangements with large national real estate chains. The prenegotiated discount is typically around ½ to 1 percent off the going rate. For example, instead of paying a 6 percent commission, you would pay 5 percent. Usually, 3 percent goes to the selling office, and 2 percent goes to the listing office.

What is the advantage?

The answer is easy: You do not have to argue with the real estate agent. Using its ability to deliver lots of sellers as clout, the company has already done the negotiating for you. You simply call up a predesignated agent who comes by and offers you the prenegotiated price. If you have ever bought a car through the American Automobile Association (AAA) or Costco, you already are familiar with a similar procedure.

This also applies to large corporations who arrange for a discount rate with major real estate agencies when transferring their employees. If you are relocating because of your job, ask your company about this.

Discount Realties

Many real estate companies will offer you a reduced commission rate without requiring your membership in a store or other organization. Typically, these discounters are found in highly competitive markets. A few years ago when the Denver, Colorado, residential real estate market was exploding, almost every agent seemed to be offering a discount. Advertisements for discounts were common in the newspapers and on television. When people went out for dinner and came back to their car, chances are a flyer would be under the windshield wiper advertising a discount broker.

At the same time in the huge Southern California market, nary a discount could be found. This was a sluggish market, and agents were holding a fairly large inventory of homes. As of this writing, the picture has changed in Southern California, where the market is now very hot. And discounters seem to be everywhere.

As these examples suggest, you're more likely to find discounters thriving in a hot market than in a lukewarm one. I'm not sure why this is so; perhaps sellers believe that when the market is cold, they need to give the agent a big commission to get a sale.

Who Are the Discounters?

Two of the biggest discount real estate firms are HelpUSell and Assist2Sell. Their franchise agencies have spread across the country. There may be one in your area. Or a completely different and new discounting office may be cropping up.

Internet discounters tend to come and go. Recently, eRealty and other local realties have been making a big splash. There are discounters now in most states.

There are also the independents. These brokerages may have several offices in a particular locale that offer services at a discount.

Backlash

In talking with discounters, I have learned that most are well aware of sellers' concerns with commission rates and foresee a trend toward lower rates. They see themselves on the crest of the wave, and many believe that in the years to come almost all real estate agents will reduce their rates.

On the other hand, full-service offices sometimes view discounters as being unfairly competitive and refuse to work on their listings, which is a disadvantage to the sellers of those properties.

How Do Discounters Work?

The original strategy for many discounters was to provide support for For-Sale-by-Owner (FSBO) sellers. They would do most of the heavy lifting including listing the property on the Multiple Listing Service (MLS) and handling the paperwork, but the owner would need to do some of the work, such as showing the property.

In general, that's no longer the case. Most discounters today claim to offer full service. They say they will provide you with the same assistance in selling your home that any other real estate company offers.

But, you may reasonably ask, how can they do this given the commission splits described in Chapter 2? Cutting the commission rate also cuts the commission dramatically for the listing office, doesn't it?

Not necessarily. Some offices, such as Assist2Sell, say they make up for it with increased volume. Some discounters use a different commission structure. They may not offer a commission at all to their salespeople, who instead work on a flat fee basis. When a house they've listed sells, they get a flat sum, which may be smaller than the commission that a full-priced agent might receive.

I've encountered several discount agencies that also pay their agents a regular paycheck, a kind of hourly or weekly stipend that is similar to a draw against sales, to help the agents budget their money on a day-to-day basis. Thus in many ways, these agents in the field resemble employees more than they do entrepreneurs. (Technically, however, they may still be independent contractors.)

Discount brokers (who own and run the office) often are more active and perform more functions than brokers in full-price offices. They may be out there listing and selling, instead of sitting back and waiting for the salespeople to bring in the deals. Indeed, the broker may act as a kind of supersalesperson and the salespeople a bit more like secretarial staff.

In many ways, the new discounters are a throwback to the old independent office where the broker handled most of the work. Now, however, the broker can work under the umbrella of a national chain and have helper salespeople.

In any event, the discount office's organization and pay structure result in a lower commission rate for you. The question is, how low?

What Is the Discount Rate?

The rate varies by:

- Area of the country
- Company
- Individual office
- Each listing

There is no "standard" discount rate. Each office will have its own rate, and sometimes the discount will depend on how difficult the agents think it will be to sell your property. The typical discount seems to be between 1 and 1.5 percent. Some offices go as high as 2.5 percent, but their agents appear to offer greatly reduced services:

Discounted Commission Structure

1.5 percent	Listing office
3.0 percent	Buyer's agent's office

Using these percentages, the seller would pay 4.5 percent. The buyer's agent's office would get the same 3 percent commission as if the home were listed at 6 percent. The listing office would absorb the full discount of 1.5 percent. The reasoning here is that the seller would want the buyer's agent's office to get the biggest chunk of the commission to induce agents to work hard to find a buyer.

In talking with discounters, I've found that many of them hope to represent both the seller *and* the buyer. In that way, they can collect the entire 4.5 percent commission. Remember, to have the best chance of selling, you need to have the entire system working for you. You need to expose your property to as many agents as possible, so that (working the odds) one may happen to have a buyer just looking for your property. Thus, having the commission at a full 3 percent for the buyer's agent makes good sense for you.

Before leaving the matter of commission structure, it's worth noting that some discounters use a different breakdown—a 50-50 split:

Alternate Discounted
Commission Split

2.5 percent   Listing office
2.5 percent   Selling Office

Here the listing and selling offices split a lower commission rate. The advantage is that the listing office is more likely to work harder since it's going to get more. The disadvantage is that other brokers may not work as hard for you because their end of the split is lower.

The focus in the rest of this chapter is on qualifying discounters. How do you decide whether an agent and a discount are right for you? The first consideration is the MLS.

Will My House Be Listed on the Multiple Listing Service?

I was driving down a street in my neighborhood and noticed a home with a discounter's For Sale sign that had the word "Exclusive" on it. I called the agent, who told me that she was the exclusive agent. No, the house was not listed on the MLS and no, at this point she was not interested in cobrokering, or cooperating and splitting the commission with other brokers. (Maybe she'd do that in a month or so if it didn't sell.) She said she felt it would sell quickly and, frankly, didn't want to share the discounted commission.

The following Sunday, I was again driving by and noticed she was holding an open house at the property, so I stopped by. The owners happened to be home and I chatted with them. They were ever so pleased with their agent. Besides giving them a discount, she was planning on holding open houses every weekend, had advertised the property in the newspaper, and had listed it, with a picture, on her company's website. They thought she was doing an exemplary job.

I wasn't so sure.

As noted, people rarely buy a home they stop to look at during an open house or in answer to an ad. Instead, agents most often sell homes by working with buyers and noticing that a specific house is just right for them. The lister is rarely the selling agent. Usually it's someone else.

That was the case here. Two months after I first noticed the home, I was driving by and saw the "Exclusive" sign had been removed and in its place was an "On the MLS" sign. Apparently the home hadn't sold, and the agent—on the tail end of a listing—had relisted it on the MLS that almost all of the agents in the area used to cobroker property. She is probably now promoting the property to other agencies as actively as she can.

Not doing this initially was a disservice to the sellers. Hoping to enrich herself, she convinced them that she could do a better job by "vest-pocketing" the listing (not sharing it). All that she ended up doing was delaying the sale for the sellers.

When listing with a discounter, beware of those who try to sell you on vest-pocketing the listing to keep it out of the hands of other brokers. It's not you, but the agent, who will likely benefit from this strategy. At a minimum, make certain that your property will be listed in the MLS. That will allow other brokers to work on it. And try to ensure that the commission paid to the selling agent is as high as possible, which will encourage other agents to show your property.

You may want to get a discount, but you certainly don't want that discount to come at the price of a slower or even no sale.

Note: A slow sale can result in a lower price. After a property has been on the market for awhile, it gets stale. Other agents assume that there must be a good reason it hasn't sold and tend to shy away from it. Thus, your best opportunity for selling occurs right after you have listed the home. Don't waste that valuable time with an agent who vest-pockets your listing.

Is Your House Listed on the Internet?

At one time, the Internet was touted as the wave of the future for selling homes. Supposedly, all sellers would list their homes directly on the Internet, and online would be the first place buyers would look.

Well, that has not come to pass, at least not yet. Nevertheless, quite a few people do check the Internet for homes for sale, so you won't want to ignore this opportunity. Make sure that your discounter provides this service.

Houses listed on the MLS often are picked up and shown on www.realtor.com and on other major websites. Sometimes there's a relatively small fee for this exposure. If there is a fee and your discounter doesn't want to pick it up, you should consider paying for it yourself.

Most real estate companies today have their own websites. If buyers want to learn more about your house before actually touring it, they can check it out online. There may be a detailed description of the amenities your home offers as well as several pictures (a video tour is also possible, but is expensive; if your agent doesn't want to pay for it, it may not be worthwhile for you to pick up the costs).

Will the Discount Company Actually Sell My House?

After the preceding caveats, you may feel a bit jittery about list-ing with a discounter. Is it realistic to worry that perhaps the company won't be able to sell your home?

Any legitimate real estate company can sell your home . . . or not. The real question should be, will you get the same kind of sale (as fast and for as much money) from a discounter as you'll get from a full-commission office?

Maybe.

A great many variables are involved. There are all the pres-sures that affect any real estate sale, such as market conditions and the show quality of your home. The capabilities of your par-ticular agent, whether full-price or discounter, also enter in. And there's the amount of commission that will go to the selling (not the discounter listing) office.

The biggest variable, however, is the speed and energy of the agency in promoting the sale of your home, mainly to other agents. If the discounter aggressively gets the word out on your home, then all else being equal, it should sell just as fast as with an agency that would charge full price. But, if your discounter wants to vest-pocket your listing (as in the earlier example) or otherwise doesn't promote it throughout the industry, your home could languish for a long time and you could get a lower price.

Have You Checked Out the Discounter?

Once you have found a discount office that will put your prop-erty on the MLS and will make a strong effort to promote it, you should check it out thoroughly in the following areas:

Checking Out the Services of Discounters

- *What assistance will they provide?* You should get this in writing. You want to be sure you understand thoroughly just what you're getting for the money you pay.

    A full-price office presumably will offer full assistance by handling every aspect of the transaction for you, from finding a buyer to transmitting the key at the close of escrow.

    You want to be sure that the discounter is offering just as much; if not, you need to know what the discounter is not providing. You should pay special attention to the following items:

    —Advertising

    —Showing the home to buyers

    —Answering phone calls about your home

    —Negotiating

    —Drawing up the sales agreement and other documents

    —Managing the escrow

- *How long a listing do they want?* Be wary of any agency that wants a listing for more than three months. If a house hasn't sold in 3 months, you need to analyze the situation. Is the market terrible? Is something intrinsically wrong with the house? Is it priced too high? Or, is there a problem with the agent?

    If you determine that there's a problem with the agent, then a listing of only three months allows you to drop that agent, and list with another. Longer listings tie you in too much.

    This is particularly true of a discounter where you may be unsure of the service the agent will actually provide.

You want to see what the agent is actually doing. And three months allows you to do this. Besides, if you like the agent and the real problem turns out to be the market, your house, or the price, you can always lower the price or make improvements and relist for another three months.

- *Is the company reliable?* It goes without saying that you should investigate any agency before listing with it. If you're wary of a discounter, but want to try it, this is certainly true. Here are some ways to examine the company's track record:

  —Has the agent always arrived when agreed, called you back promptly, followed through on everything as promised? While behavior before the listing is not a guarantee, generally speaking it reflects behavior afterward. If the agent is hard to reach, doesn't show when agreed, and doesn't follow through before the listing, why would anything be different afterward?

The following should be done for any agent before listing:

  —Have you called the real estate department in your state to see if any complaints have been lodged against the company? Many states operate websites to facilitate just such inquiries.

  —Have you checked with the Better Business Bureau in your area? Just being a member often indicates a company is anxious to please its customers.

  —Have you checked with your local district attorney's office to see if the company is under investigation? While this may seem extreme, it is practical advice. Isn't it better to find out that the district attorney is preparing to file a complaint against an agency before you list than after you have signed a contract?

—Are the agent and the company members of the National Association of Realtors (NAR)? Discounters should belong to the biggest national trade group.

Making the Final Decision

Should you go with a discounter?

Ultimately, you have to ask yourself, why not? Assuming everything checks out, as noted, what have you got to lose and what have you got to gain? If there's more to be gained than lost, then the discounter makes a lot of sense.

A word needs to be said, however, on my favorite topic—choosing by person, instead of by company or even by price. In real estate, the person you are dealing with counts the most. Not the broker, the company, or the price.

If you have found a terrific real estate agent, then stick with that person. On the other hand, if you have doubts about an agent who is offering you a discount, be careful. You might end up being penny-wise and pound-foolish.

5

Negotiating Rebates and Reduced Commissions

Although listing your property with a discount broker has some advantages, as described in Chapter 4, you may prefer to use an agent you know, perhaps a friend or someone recommended by a person you trust. Or you may choose to go to a national chain or an independent broker who normally does full commission work. However, you still want to negotiate a lower commission rate because you know that although the commission rate has remained unchanged in the past 5 years, agents today are getting far higher commissions as a result of skyrocketing property values. Or perhaps you simply feel that a 6 percent or so rate is intrinsically too high.

Whatever the reason, you are now faced with negotiating a lower rate from someone who isn't coming to you prepared to offer a discount. Can you do it?

Possibly. Just remember that the agent may refuse to accept a lower commission rate under any conditions. If so, you'll just have to accept that and agree to the higher rate or go elsewhere.

Fair-minded agents will hear you out, may offer their own arguments to justify the commission rate they want, and may even agree to charge less if you are suitably persuasive. It probably won't hurt to try although you may risk alienating an agent who is sensitive to the issue.

When to Negotiate the Lower Rate

There are basically three times when you can effectively negotiate a reduced rate of commission:

1. When you sign a listing agreement
2. When you sign a sales agreement
3. When you purchase your next home

When You Sign a Listing Agreement

The moment you begin discussing a reduced commission rate with an agent, you're likely to find yourself in an adversarial position. This is not to say that you don't like the agent or that the agent doesn't like you. You may be the best of friends. It's just that for now, your self-interests diverge. You want to pay the least you can. And, of course, the agent wants you to pay the most.

You happen to know (from talking with other agents), that the going rate in your area is 6 percent. But you've found an agent you like (we discuss qualifying the agent at the end of this chapter) and want to offer only 5 or perhaps 4 percent. How can you ask the agent to work for a reduced commission (assuming that he or she doesn't offer to do so) and maintain friendly, or at least business-cordial relations?

One way is to get it out on the table by saying that you're interested in a reduced commission rate listing. If you state this intent firmly (as in, you'll only offer a reduced rate), you let the agent know your plans immediately. Then the agent may acquiesce, and the rest of the negotiations can focus on how low it will be. Or, the agent may refuse to consider a lower rate and try to convince you to pay a higher rate. Or, the agent can simply say, "Good-bye."

This up-front approach is quick and straightforward, but it is abrupt and not suitable for nonassertive sellers. Another approach is to let the agent bring up the matter of commission after you've completed the agent interview process and have told the agent you want to list. The agent brings out the listing form, begins filling it out, and notes that the commission will be 6 percent. You reply, "Nope, 4 percent."

This will have the effect of suddenly bringing all conversation to a dead halt. The agent will look at you as though you've suddenly grown two stalks of celery out of the top of your head and will probably repeat the 6 percent mantra.

At that point, you will need to explain why you think this commission rate is too high and why you want to pay less. (Be sure to read the following chapters on arguments for different listing structures.)

The advantage of waiting to discuss the commission until the agent brings it up is that by then you and the agent have invested a lot of time, conversation, and energy in the project. At this point, both of you will want to make the listing work, somehow. Hence, you are more likely to engage in serious negotiations. (Also, by now you may have had some frank discussion of the agent's qualifications without the matter of fee getting in the way.)

When You Sign a Sales Agreement

Assume that you have signed a listing agreement to pay a 6 percent commission. The agent has cobrokered the house and put it on the Multiple Listing Service (MLS). Now a different salesperson has found a buyer, but you are reluctant to accept the offer. It is for less than you are asking, and you feel that your home is worth thousands more than this offer.

Or perhaps instead of offering a lower price, it asks you to put on a new roof, and you don't think there's anything wrong with the roof.

Or . . . ? There could be any number of reasons that you simply don't want to sign the agreement. Your agent and the buyer's agent, meanwhile, are pressing you hard to sign. After all, they don't get a commission unless you do.

So, you say to them, "Okay, if you want to make this deal so badly, chip in part of your commission. If you cut your commission $5,000 [or $2,000 or $7,000 or whatever], then I'll cut my demands a bit and the deal will be made."

It is important to understand that even if you've signed a listing agreement for a set rate of commission such as 6 percent, there is nothing to prevent an agent from later reducing that rate. (You can't cut the rate, but the agent can.)

Now the ball is in the agent's court. He or she can agree to cut the commission to make the deal. Or he can simply say, "Nope," and you just won't sell the home.

The agent is going to try to gauge just how sincere you are. An agent who thinks this is a ploy on your part—that you really want to sell and are just trying to make more money on the deal—is likely to stonewall and refuse.

On the other hand, if the agent senses that you're sincere, won't budge, and don't care if you lose the deal at the price and terms currently offered, then maybe, just maybe, the agent(s) will cut the commission to make it all work.

Does this happen every time? Nope.

Does it happen fairly often? I believe so, from what I've seen.

Agents aren't stupid, and they know all the old maxims: A *bird in the hand is worth two in the bush; No deal, no meal;* and *Half a loaf is better than no loaf at all.*

Before letting a solid sale slip by, some agents will throw in a portion of their commission to make it happen.

In fact, I was just talking with a woman who was astounded to see this happen when she was selling her home in Pasadena, California. It was a $650,000 property (it's a high-priced area), and the buyer and seller were $12,000 apart. Roughly a $45,000 total commission was involved, and the agents huddled and agreed to throw in the difference to make it happen. They reduced their commission from 6 percent to 5 percent.

This is, in effect, playing hardball. And the results are going to be mixed. Sometimes it will work, and sometimes it won't. That's why I don't advocate this as a general strategy for getting a commission rate cut. If the situation develops, go with it. Just don't plan in advance on it happening.

When You Purchase Your Next Home

Finally, there's the matter of giving a real estate agent two deals instead of one. In most situations, not only do we need to sell our present house, we also need to buy a new one. If the new home is going to be in the same area, why not deal with the same agent? After all, if you liked the agent when selling your property, you should like that agent equally well when you buy.

This gives the agent a big advantage. As the lister on the sale of your home and the buyer's agent on the purchase of your next home, the agent in effect has a round-trip deal—a sale and a purchase (of two homes).

Thus, you offer to work with the agent both ways, provided you get a reduced commission rate when you sell. (You can negotiate this at the time you list your property, or at the time it sells, or when you're ready to buy.)

Many agents will cut their rate because of what you offer. However, they may not be willing to cut it *until* you actually make your next purchase. Thus, they may agree that when your home sells, you'll pay them the full commission. However, when you buy your next home, they will rebate to you a portion of that first commission, thus effectively reducing the rate you paid.

Be sure you get this straight. You don't get the cut when you sell. Instead, you get a rebate when you buy.

Are rebates legal?

It is illegal to pay a commission to anyone who is not a licensed agent. That probably means you. However, there is normally nothing to prevent an agent from reducing a portion of the commission paid by the seller. Check it out.

These, then, are the times when you'll most likely want to negotiate a reduced commission. But, there's still the matter of how to handle the negotiations. Here are some simple rules that may help.

Negotiating the Commission

The following rules will make it easier for you to negotiate openly and successfully with your agent. Not all apply every time. But often one or more of them can make the difference:

- *Know how much your agent actually makes.* Agents can't cut the commission below what they make. Know your agent's split with the broker. Know the split between the buying and selling offices. Ask about the franchise fee and any transaction costs. If you're not sure what these figures are, ask. The agent should be willing to provide this information; after all, you're paying the bill. Remember, don't ask for more than your agent can give.
- *Find out your agent's relationship with the realty office/broker.* Can the agent negotiate the commission rate for the office? Or can only the broker do that? If the broker is the only person authorized to negotiate commission, then you're talking to the wrong person. Make an appointment to see the broker.
- *Keep it at a business level.* You don't want or need to be the agent's best friend. You simply need the agency's services, just as that office needs your listing. Asking the

agent to lower a commission as a personal favor won't get you anywhere (unless the agent happens to owe you a personal favor) and will tend to muddy the waters.

- *Keep the negotiations going.* If you and the agent get angry and stalk away, there's no listing. And no lower commission for you. Keep things civil and friendly, at all times.
- *Respect the agent.* Remember, you want this person to end up on your side, promoting your house, getting you the best price. If you knock the agent, then even if you end up with a lower commission rate, you might also end up with an agent who really doesn't like you and won't work hard for you.
- *Don't expect the agent to agree, at least not right away.* At some point, the agent may simply say, "It may be better if you list with someone else. I know what I'm worth, and I won't accept a lower commission." If this is the agent's final word, be willing to accept it. Your final word may be that you're not willing to pay the high freight the agent is demanding. Agree to disagree. If you end the negotiations cordially, the agent may surprise you by calling back in a day or so to propose a compromise.
- *Consider paying the full commission.* If you want a particular agent and he or she seems to offer the best opportunity for a quick sale at your price, it's probably worth it.

Be Prepared to Interview Many Agents

Agents come from a culture where they expect, or at least hope, to dictate the commission rate. You're trying to change that arrangement. For some agents, this will be particularly hard to accept. They may think that you're odd or a troublemaker or difficult person to work with. They may not want to handle your listing at all. Real estate tends to attract conservative salespeople, so your new ideas are unlikely to have immediate, wide appeal.

You may have to repeat your request for a lower commission structure on more than a single agent, perhaps on several agents, before you find one who is willing to cooperate with you. It resembles the process that is used to sell a home. You try to get your home in front of as many buyers as possible so that you can find the one who really wants it. The same strategy may be necessary to obtain a reduced commission rate. You may have to approach a lot of agents with the idea, before you find one who is knowledgeable and agreeable.

It's Your Right

It's important to understand that you have the right to negotiate the commission rate at which you will list your property. I've listened to agents who, when confronted with a seller's request to negotiate the commission, mutter a few unkind words under their breath and intimate that they must be dealing with some sort of lower life form. They then go on to indicate that they work hard for their money, they know what their efforts are worth, and they want you to realize that you're taking food out of the mouths of their children by even suggesting a lower rate.

Don't be put off by an agent who tries to intimidate you, who suggests that you can't negotiate the commission (the commission is *completely* negotiable), who says that someone who offers you a lower rate couldn't possibly provide the services you need, that the only way to sell your house is to pay the high(est) rate being demanded.

All you are requesting is a fair and equitable discussion about the fee. If you were hiring an employee (or were being hired), you would expect nothing less. An agent who is unwilling to openly discuss the commission probably doesn't really want your business. On the other hand, a creative agent who respects your perspective may give you the best sales assistance you've ever had, and at the best price.

Qualifying Your Agent

Note: You can perform this task before or after you've discussed commission.

To begin, it's important to get your head straight. In hiring an agent, you are like an employer. Have you ever hired someone in the course of your regular work? If so, then you've got a rough idea of what it means to negotiate with an agent. (If you've never hired an employee, chances are that someone has hired you—just switch places around the table and imagine you're sitting in the chair of the person who interviewed you.)

When you hire someone, at least three issues are at stake:

1. How competent is the agent (can this agent do the job)?
2. How willing is the agent to work?
3. How much should the agent be paid? (which we've already covered)

Salary never is (or should never be) the sole consideration. Whether you hired janitors or nuclear physicists, if they were unable or unwilling to do the job, what would you have gained, even if you paid them pennies? Similarly, if you paid them millions and they were still unable or unwilling to do the work, you would lose.

Sellers who don't understand this truth often mistakenly focus strictly on the price—the commission—and go after the agent who offers them the lowest rate. In taking this approach, they risk ending up with a lazy agent or even an incompetent who lists their home and then disappears, never to be heard from again. And as a result, the property may languish without buyers.

Your goal is to sell your property. Although you want to pay the lowest commission rate possible, a low rate and no sale is not acceptable. Therefore, you must always consider the competence and willingness of the agent who will be working for you.

How Competent Is the Agent?

You need to determine that the agent can, indeed, handle the sale of your property. If the agent doesn't have the necessary qualifications, even one dollar is too much to pay for a commission.

How do you know whether your agent is competent?

While there are no guarantees, certain telltale signs will help you here. Conduct an interview, just as if you were hiring an employee. Ask your would-be agent the following five questions and be guided by the answers:

1. *Are you a Realtor?* Most people confuse the terms "agent" and "Realtor" in the erroneous belief that they have the same meaning. An agent is any person licensed to sell real estate. A Realtor is a member of the National Association of Realtors (NAR), a trade group dedicated to promoting excellence in the field.

Belonging to this organization is a must requirement for an agent. It doesn't guarantee that the agent is honest or knowledgeable, but it indicates that the agent is licensed and has, at the least, joined the largest national trade group for the profession.

2. *How long have you been selling real estate?* Experience counts. Agents can't learn how to sell real estate from a book. Getting a license simply means that they have absorbed the basic real property laws of a particular state. The only way to learn is to be on the front lines making deals. The more deals that agents make, the more they learn about the different situations (crises) that come up and how to deal with them successfully.

You want an experienced agent who can immediately step in with an answer that will work for you if a problem comes up. Look for an agent who has been in business for at least 5 years— 10 years is better.

3. *Were you active all that time?* This question can confuse some sellers. In most businesses, holding a job in an office means you're working full time, 9 to 5. In real estate, however, many agents are in reality only part-timers. They come to the office, sit in a chair, look at the new listings on the computer, go out to lunch, and take the afternoon off to play golf.

Are they making a living selling real estate? Probably not. They may receive a retirement benefit from another profession or have some other outside source of income. I've known many military men who served their 20 years, retired fairly young, and now sell real estate. The same can be true for teachers. Some of these part-timers are terrific agents, the best in the business. But others have little incentive to excel and just go through the motions.

Many real estate offices are guilty of cultivating part-time agents. Some offices have a policy stating that agents must sell at least one or perhaps two properties a year. Unless agents sell multimillion-dollar properties, they can't earn a living from so few sales. The office, however, may find it is profitable to retain these agents, who only get 50 percent of the commission and bring in a couple of deals a year. An agent I met the other day was distraught because her office had finally dumped her, after she had failed to bring in a single sale for 13 months. This part-time agent may be less likely to service you as well as an agent who has been doing a deal every month. An active agent is likely to be a more knowledgeable agent.

Ask any agents you interview how many deals they have made in the past 12 months. If the answer is only one or two, look elsewhere. If it's half a dozen or a dozen, keep talking.

4. *What is your commission split with your broker?* There's an unwritten rule in social discourse that says you must never directly ask people how much money they make. It is considered uncouth.

Asking agents about the commission split is sort of like asking how much money they make. However, before you hire someone to represent you as an agent, you need to know whether the person is successful. Never mind being couth! Never mind that the agent drives a late model luxury car and dresses well. You can buy almost any car for so much a month, and inexpensive knockoffs in discount stores easily mimic top brands of clothes.

Be upfront. No, you're not asking to see their tax returns and, yes, they might lie. But I've found that most agents tell the truth about this. (They are so shocked that they just blurt it out!) They may say they get a standard 50/50 split. Or perhaps it's an advantageous 60/40 split. Or an outstanding 75/25 or 80/20 split.

The percentages are important because the better the split, the more successful the agent. Agents receive higher splits as a reward for bringing in more business. An agent who is only getting 50/50 probably is either a beginner or a mediocre agent. Likewise, an agent who is getting a 75/25 or higher split is usually very active and highly successful.

5. *May I see the last few homes you have sold? (Ask this only of an agent you're almost ready to hire.)* An agent who is successful should be willing to drive you by recent sales. Most agents will be proud to do this. Now ask to talk to the buyers of the home (at which time, you can ask how long ago the sale took place, how satisfied the buyer was, and whether the buyer was related to the agent—not a brother-in-law you hope!). You're sitting in the car right in front of the house. How much of an effort is it to drop in and say hello to a former satisfied client?

Agents may be surprised at your request, but if they really did do a good job, they should be on excellent terms with the former client. Agents are used to popping in and talking to people, so it should be no big deal. If they aren't willing to let you talk to at least one of their last three clients, there may have been problems with those transactions.

How Willing Is the Agent to Work?

This may seem a strange question, once you've qualified the agent as to competence. However, an agent who may be perfectly happy to work for a full 6 percent commission may be less happy to do the work for a lower commission, say 4 or 5 percent.

The agent may grudgingly accept a lower rate, sign you up, dump you on the MLS, and never see you again. You may not get the assistance you need because you're offering a reduced commission.

This is similar to the ploy that a few agents use when signing up a person who wants too much for a property. The agent knows the price is too high and that the property will never sell as listed. This agent, unprofessionally, takes the listing, puts it on the MLS, but does no work selling it in the hope that after a month or two, the seller will realize that the price is too high and will then drop it to a lower, more reasonable level. At that point, the agent will begin actively to sell the home. (A strictly ethical agent will inform the seller at the outset that the price is too high, state what the agent believes is the correct price, and attempt to list the property only at that price.)

You want an agent who is enthusiastic and willing to work on your home no matter what the commission rate is. How do you determine if the agent is excited about selling your property?

Ask.

Three Questions to Determine an Agent's Enthusiasm

1. *How will you market my home?* The willing agent will immediately begin talking about all the ways to promote the sale of your property. There will be a sign, a flyer, advertising, agent open houses, caravans, faxes, and phone calls to other agents.

Enthusiastic agents don't hold anything back, but devote their full energies to selling your home. And their enthusiasm is visible as they begin describing all the things they will do for you.

2. *Do you resent being paid a lower commission rate?* It is best to get these ill feelings out in the open. You may have pressured agents to get a reduced commission rate. They may have accepted. Now you want to know if they accepted because you convinced them of the wisdom of that decision or reluctantly went along because they wanted just to get another listing.

Agents aren't likely to come right out and say they resent it, but they may begin explaining why you've made a mistake in demanding a lower rate. And along the way, they may let you know that they plan to offer a lesser level of assistance than you want or need.

As noted, you get what you pay for. So be sure you're paying for what you expect to get.

3. *How long will it take to sell my home?* No one can answer that question. However, good agents will give you a candid opinion. They may say that given current market conditions and the price you're asking, it could take a week, or a month, or 6 months.

What you're looking for is more than an opinion—you want enthusiasm. You want a positive answer that suggests the agent is excited about working hard to get a quick sale.

The last thing you want to hear is that the lower commission means it will to take longer to sell your home. If that's truly the case, then either you need a more enthusiastic agent or you need to readjust the commission rate.

Only after you've qualified your agent in both competency and enthusiasm, should you consider yourself ready to go forward with a reduced commission rate.

What about a Flat Fee?

Here's a revolutionary idea: Instead of paying the agent a commission based on the selling price, why not pay the agent a set fee regardless of the sales price?

In this chapter I suggest several commission payment options that are not widely used or accepted, yet. But, there's no reason the buyer and seller cannot negotiate or accept such arrangements. Actually, the option of a flat fee is not as revolutionary as it may sound. When you have surgery, the surgeon usually charges a flat fee for the operation regardless of possible complications. If you hire a mechanic to fix your car, you want to pay either a set fee or an hourly rate for labor. Why should it be so different for real estate agents?

Most likely, the reason agents are commissioned is that years ago they were often hired on the basis of how much money they could get for a property. Today's scientific appraisal methods did not exist 70 years ago (or longer), and estimating the value of a property was problematic.

Today, the standard method of determining residential property values is by comparison. There's hardly a seller (or buyer) anywhere who doesn't get a comparative market analysis (CMA) from a real estate agent. It compares recent sales of comparable properties in the neighborhood. From the selling prices of the "comps," it's fairly easy to deduce what the subject property is likely to bring on the market. Often it's possible to nail it down to within a few hundred dollars.

Finding comps 70 years ago wasn't so simple (there was no computerized system to do the search). And as a result, determining value was also harder. As recently as 40 years ago, agents regularly were taught to use reconstruction costs as a good method of determining value. (They would determine a price for the lot, calculate how much it would cost to build the current house on it, add the two together, and get the current value.)

No agents use this method now, except for new construction. And even then, comps are often more important.

Years ago when determining property values was imprecise, agents and sellers would put their heads together to come up with a price they thought was reasonable. The figure was more often on the high side than on the low side. It was up to the agent to find a buyer at the higher price.

The incentive was that the higher the price the agent could persuade a buyer to pay, the bigger the commission the agent would get. Contrarily, the lower an offer, the less money the agent would make. The agent had a vested interest in getting a high price for the seller.

Autos Have Sticker Prices

As a comparison, think of the way dealers sold new cars before the federal government required manufacturers to put sticker prices on their vehicles. To get a higher commission, salespeople would try to get the highest possible price for cars, even if it was more than the manufacturer quoted. Many buyers were buffaloed into paying far too much.

Auto salespeople still sell on commission and still try to beef up their commissions by getting buyers to pay the highest possible prices for new and used cars. However, with sticker prices clearly listed on new cars and with *Kelly Blue Book* values and dealer invoices readily available over the Internet, the range of prices is much smaller. Most buyers today *know* what the car is worth before they even walk into the dealership.

Similarly, the buying and selling of houses has changed. Using computerized listing systems, both buyers and sellers can quickly learn what their home should bring on the market. There is generally a range within which a house that shows well will bring more than one that shows badly, but even this variance can be included in the price calculation.

Further, different agents usually represent the buyer and the seller. The buyer's agent knows as much (or should) about house values as the seller's agent, which diminishes the chances of big swings in price. (We're not talking here about bargain hunting or buying a home for far less than market value, which is a specialized area of real estate.)

Except in hot markets, listing agents today are less likely to view a commission as an incentive to bring in a higher offer than they did in the distant past. At 6 percent, the full commission on a $300,000 home is $18,000. If it sells for $310,000, the fee increases only to $18,600. Considering the breakdown in commission between buyer's agent and seller's agent, between broker and salesperson, that $600 additional is likely to be worth only about $150 at the agent's level (see Chapter 2). How hard do you think an agent is going to work to sell the property for an additional $10,000 for you, when that agent's share is only $150? It is hard enough just getting buyer and seller together at any price.

Exceptions occur in very hot markets. Some agents then use sales tricks to encourage offers. They may list the house at a low price to produce a buying frenzy of offers or set up range listings, where the price is a range instead of a fixed figure. A creative agent can significantly boost the price that sellers get for their property. Tagging the commission to the sales price can make sense here. (See also Chapter 7.)

Lawyers Offer a Variety of Fee Schedules

Another helpful comparison is the one between attorneys and their clients. Many attorneys offer their clients several fee structures. They have an hourly fee based on the amount of work the lawyer has to do. There may be a charge of $150 an hour (or more) to prepare a trust or a will or to handle probate. An alternative set fee structure is to offer services for a single flat fee. Putting together a trust with a will might be $1,000 regardless of the time spent.

Attorneys also sometimes offer contingency pricing. Essentially, the client pays nothing. The attorney foots all the costs of the litigation including investigators, court appearances, and filing fees. The attorney, however, gets a commission based on the ultimate settlement (for example, one-third of the settlement). Thus, if the settlement is $100,000, the attorney might get $33,000. But, if it's a million-dollar settlement, the fee will be $330,000.

The client's incentive is that it costs nothing to pursue the lawsuit. The attorney's incentive is that the legal fee is directly tied to the size of the settlement. And this usually works to the client's advantage because the more the attorney receives, the more there should also be for the client. (Sometimes expenses are deducted from the client's share, which is a separate issue.)

What Am I Likely to Gain from Commissioning the Agent?

As a seller, you need to ask yourself, How much incentive am I providing by offering the agent a commission? Will the commission likely result in a higher price, and hence more money, for me? Or am I likely to get the same amount regardless?

If I ask $300,000, will I get a higher price if I pay the agent a commission of 6 percent, or a flat fee of $18,000? (Remember, 6 percent of $300,000 is $18,000.) Will the agent who receives a commission instead of a flat rate try to find a buyer willing to pay more?

In asking several agents this question, the reply I received is that in a cold market, they might prefer the flat fee, since the house is likely to sell for less than asking price. However, in a hot market, the house possibly might sell for more than the list price, hence the percentage of sale would be preferable. They pointed out, however, that the seller who offers a percentage commission stands to gain if the house sells for less. What if the house ultimately sells for $250,000? At 6 percent, the commission is only $15,000. That's $3,000 in savings over a flat fee of $18,000. On the other hand, if you offer a flat fee of $18,000 and the house sells for $350,000, you've saved yourself $3,000 in extra commission costs over a 6 percent rate.

Flat Fee Agents

Today, there are agents in some areas who will handle certain parts of the deal for a predetermined flat fee which varies according to the work performed. For example, they may write up the sales agreement, handle the disclosures, or work the escrow for you. These are called "fee-for-service" agents. If you locate one of these agents, there is no reason you cannot ask them to, similarly, handle the whole transaction for you for a flat fee.

––––––––––

Note: Fee-for-service agents are less prevalent than in the past simply because of the fact that their liability in case something goes wrong tends to be as great whether they perform one simple service or handle the entire deal. Yet, they only get a small compensation for, say, helping you with disclosures, as opposed to a big commission for taking care of the entire sale. On the other hand, if you offer a large flat fee to do it all, they could be very receptive.

Check the local phone book and advertisements in local papers for fee-for-service agents that might be in your area. See Chapter 11 for more details on this subject.

The next decision involves the amount of the fee that the seller should offer to an agent as an alternative to a commission.

How High to Set the Fee?

If the fee is just 6 percent or 5 percent or whatever of the selling price, then it's no fee at all. It's just a commission. On the other hand, while an agent will want the fee to be as large as possible, the sellers will want it to be as small as possible. What is fair?

One method is to consider the median sales price of a home in your area. Let's say it is $200,000. (It is actually less than that nationally, as of this writing, but it may be higher or lower in your area—any agent should be able to provide this information.)

Further, the typical commission in your area may be 6 percent. That means $12,000 is the median commission. If an agent is willing to sell a $200,000 home for a $12,000 commission, why not the same amount for a $300,000 home? Or a million-dollar one? If the fee is large enough to cover the agent's costs for the basic $200,000 home, why not for the more expensive property?

One argument is that additional costs could be involved in promoting a higher priced property. If the agent points these out, you may want to increase your fee to cover those extra costs. Nevertheless, a flat fee might be arranged that would cover the agent's expenses plus profit. And it's probably going to be less than the commission rate on high-price homes.

There is also the matter of homes that are priced below the $200,000 level. What about a $100,000 house? Should the seller also pay a $12,000 fee when a 6 percent commission is only $6,000?

I've always believed what's good for the goose is good for the gander. If you're an advocate of a fixed fee, then whatever you set as the minimum fee for selling your home is what you should pay, regardless of the price, higher or *lower*. (I'm sure that sellers of low-price homes are not going to be happy with me here. If so, remember, this is just one of several proposals for new fee structures. And, you can always list the conventional way as a percentage commission described in this book.)

Agents also may not be happy because many assume that the income they'll get from the business comes from averaging the commissions for all the houses they sell. For every $100,000 house that they get a commission on, they'll probably also get a commission on a $300,000 house. Overall, the commissions average out.

With a flat fee structure, the average should remain roughly the same. The agent would be getting more for low-price homes and less for high-price ones.

Should the Fee Be Paid Even if the Home Isn't Sold?

Certainly the agent should receive some fee. After all, whether or not the home is sold, the agent puts forth money, time, and effort. There are those weekends spent holding open houses, there are caravans to organize and the time and effort spent contacting other agents. There are expenses for advertising, signage, and flyers. And most agents would argue that all those expenses are factored into the current commission rate structure. If you take away that commission and substitute a fee, there has to be some method for paying those expenses even when the home doesn't sell.

Is There a Consolation Fee?

In many businesses, contracts include a kind of consolation award or fee. If a magazine "hires" me to write an article on the real estate field and offers to pay me a flat fee of $1,000 for the article, there's also usually a consolation or "kill" fee. If, for whatever reason, the magazine does not use the story after I have put forth the work of writing it, the magazine will pay me 10 to 25 percent of the fee for the work I've expended—$100 to $250 in this case.

Similarly, if you take your boat into a shop to have the engine fixed, the mechanic may charge $75 (or whatever) to check it out. If you subsequently decide to have the shop do the work, the money goes toward the cost of repairs. If, however, you decide not to do the work, you still owe the money.

If you think about it, it's only fair. In the case of a flat fee for listing a home, something similar could apply. An agent who puts forth the effort for 3 months (or however long) to sell the property and is unsuccessful might still receive $1,000 to $2,500 or whatever. Many salespeople who sign up as buyer's agents try to put such a fee onto their buyer's agreement.

What about Buyer's Agents?

When you list your home with an agent, you expect the agent to show you loyalty and dedication in finding a buyer. Many buyers, however, are now signing up with agents who offer them loyalty and dedication in finding just the right home for them. These salespeople are called buyer's agents.

Buyer's agents frequently work with a buyer under the assumption that they will split the commission with a seller's agent. But some buyer's agents demand that the buyer sign an agreement to pay them separately if they are unable to split the seller's agent's commission. They may also insist on a consolation fee if the buyer eventually does not buy a property through them. (The buyer might be fickle, might decide not to buy after all, or might look in a different area—meaning that the agent would have spent time, effort, and money for nothing.)

If buyer's agents are already collecting a consolation fee, why not seller's agents?

What about an Hourly Fee?

It works for attorneys—why not agents?

Why not pay your agent, say, $50 an hour to sell your home? In the long run, it might save you thousands . . . or not!

For one thing, attorneys are set up to bill by the hour. They have itemized time sheets, often computerized, that show exactly how much time they spend on each client's case. This would be something new for nearly all agents.

Agents might object to the extra paperwork. On the other hand, they would know they were getting paid regardless of whether the home sold. (Attorneys usually get paid regardless of the outcome of a legal case.) Many agents might jump at the chance.

What if the Agent Refuses to Work for a Set Fee?

Flat fees for listing and selling are uncommon because most agents are familiar with and trust the old commission method. Also, since sellers rarely challenge the old commission system, there's little incentive for change.

Agents, like anyone else, can be reasonable people and will listen to you if you offer a listing fee structure that makes sense. If your structure offers agents far less than they can make by listing your neighbor's home, they will most likely simply listen and leave. But if your flat fee structure is high enough and includes incentives such as a consolation fee or an hourly rate, it might be appealing. And the agent may have suggestions for restructuring the fee that interest you.

Setting the fee for a listing is a matter of negotiation. If you don't make an offer and get it out on the table, you will never have the possibility of its being accepted.

Basing the Commission Rate on the Sale Price

Here's another revolutionary idea—base the rate of the commission more directly on the price received. No, it's not commonly done . . . yet.

Think of it this way: A theatrical agent has two responsibilities to clients: to get them gigs and to see that they receive the highest possible rate for their services. Real estate agents have a similar task: to find buyers for their listings and to get sellers the highest possible price for their properties.

Under the current commission structure, however, there's relatively little incentive to bring sellers a higher price. As we've seen, if the agent gets a straight 6 percent commission, the fee for selling a home at a price of $300,000 amounts to $18,000. But, at $310,000 (a sizable increase for the seller), the commission is $18,600. While the seller gets a $10,000 price boost, the agent only gets $600 more, and that may have to be split four ways or more. Where's the incentive to get the seller more money? The incentive is simply to sell the home.

But, you can increase your agent's incentive to bring you more money. One way to accomplish this is to tie the commission rate more closely to the selling price of the home.

The Net Listing

This type of listing is as old as the concept of agency (having an agent act as your representative). It has been used for hundreds of years, most recently in the sale of bare land. However, because of its potential for abuse, it has been in considerable disrepute of late. Nevertheless, if you understand a net listing and have proper safeguards, it's a way to sell your property and save thousands on the commission. Here's how a basic net listing works:

You tell a real estate agent that you want a certain *net* out of the sale of your property. Perhaps you want $200,000. Then, everything that the agent gets over $200,000 belongs to the agent. Everything that the agent gets under $200,000 is yours.

In a basic net listing, there is no commission rate based on a sales price. Instead, there is a demarcation point. Above the net line, the agent gets it all; below the line, you get it all.

Basic Net Listing Example

After careful examination of comps, you feel that your home is worth $400,000. You would feel very comfortable with that amount, if you could get it. So you offer an agent this proposition: Any amount that the agent gets below $400,000 is yours. No commission will be paid on it. Any amount above $400,000 is the agent's—none of it goes to you:

- If the home sells for an even $400,000, then you get all the money and pay no commission.
- If the home sells for $390,000, you still get it all with no commission.
- If the home sells for $415,000, then you get your $400,000 and the agent gets $15,000.
- If the home sells for $500,000, you still only get $400,000, but the agent gets $100,000.

Net listings present some interesting possibilities. You might get all your money. But, should you guess wrong about the price, the agent could stand to make far more than a standard commission. If your research on comps is flawed, it can become a crapshoot.

Making It Easier for the Agent

Few agents, however, will take your bet if you set your net line at the likely top price of the property ($400,000 in our example). They realize that the chances are remote that they will locate a buyer willing to pay more than the asking price (assuming it's close to market value). Hence, you probably won't find a taker for your listing. And, if you do, that agent is unlikely to find you buyers for anything approaching your net line, because there's nothing (or little) in it for the agent. Thus, you might lose out on potential sales unless you lower your net line. Say you will accept a net of $385,000. Everything below that amount is yours; everything above it is the agent's. Now the net is $15,000 below market, and since there's a good chance that it will sell at market, the agent has a reasonable incentive. And if it sells above market, the reward will be even greater.

You may be saying, why take $15,000 of your own money off the table? The reason is that it never was on the table. If you had paid a straight 6 percent commission on a $400,000 price, you would have paid $24,000. Here, you're saving thousands . . . plus energizing your agent. Sometimes it's better to get half a pie than no pie at all.

Splitting the Profit

There are many possible variations of the net listing. One involves splitting the profit with the agent.

Here you list the property for a low rate of commission, up to a net price. After the net price, you and the agent split whatever comes in.

You might list the property at 3 percent up to $385,000. Any amount over $385,000 is split between you and the agent.

Modified Net Listing Example

- The property sells for $385,000. You pay the agent 3 percent or $11,550.
- The property sells for $400,000. You pay the agent 3 percent up to $385,000 ($11,550) plus half of the difference ($7,500) for a total of $19,000.
- The property sells for $415,000. You pay the agent 3 percent up to $385,000 ($11,550) plus half of the difference ($15,000) for a total of $26,550.

Notice that as the price goes higher, the amount that the agent receives moves up very rapidly as well. At a sales price of $415,000, you would have been better off having listed for a straight 6 percent ($24,900). The higher the price goes, the worse your situation becomes compared with a straight percentage listing.

Drawbacks to the Net Listing

You Might Lose Money

Remember, it is a gamble, at worst, a crapshoot. It only works to the seller's advantage if the seller can accurately gauge the property's likely selling price. If it sells for much more than the seller's net, then the seller will lose money and the agent will profit. If it sells for much less, then the seller makes out and the agent suffers. Often, it is impossible to know with any surety what your home may sell for. You may think it's worth $400,000 based on comps. But a quick turn in the market and a spate of hungry buyers could boost the price, and you'd lose out on that extra profit.

You Might Structure the Listing Badly

Besides setting your net at the wrong price, you could pay the agent too large a commission on the downside and/or too high a split on the upside. These are all negotiable figures. In the preceding example, the agent received 3 percent. Perhaps that was too much . . . or not enough. Also, we split the difference with the agent on the upside. Perhaps a more realistic split was 60/40 or 70/30 going either way.

Calculating the right downside commission and upside split can be difficult. If you do it wrong, you may lose money, the agent may become dissatisfied and not spend time on your property, and/or it may simply not sell.

You Could Get Cheated

This is probably the most dire outcome. In the past, a few agents abused the net listing. They would browbeat the sellers into coming up with a low net price. Then they'd sell the property for tens of thousands of dollars more than the net, never telling the seller the actual sales price. The agent won big, the seller lost big.

Because of this and other abuses, many real estate regulatory agencies frown on the net listing. Real estate codes in many states now require agents to inform the seller of the actual selling price of the property and the amount the agent receives. Sometimes the seller must agree in writing to the amount the agent makes, regardless of what is stated on the listing contract. (In special cases, that amount may be restricted.)

To protect yourself in a net listing, make sure that you know the sales price and are happy with all the terms of the deal. It's one thing to gamble and lose. It's quite another to be cheated.

Who Should Use a Net Listing

Net listings are not for everyone. In the past, they were primarily tools for sophisticated investors, often involving bare land or commercial or industrial properties.

Today, many home sellers are becoming increasingly sophisticated, and some are advanced investors in real estate. If you are in this latter category, you may want to consider a net listing.

Regardless of your experience, I strongly urge you to have a competent attorney review any net listing agreement (and any other listing contract, for that matter) and explain it thoroughly to you before you sign.

The Multirate Commission

Here's another idea whose time may be coming.

In most cases, agents' listing agreements specify the commission rate. It might be 4 percent or 6 percent or whatever. No matter what price the buyers come in at, the rate remains the same. (The amount of the commission goes up with the price, but not by much.) This is something that agents are familiar with and understand. To encourage agents to bring in a higher offer, why not add an incentive of a higher rate, or at least a bonus, instead of just the single-rate commission.

In its simplest form, this commission structure operates over a variety of rates. There might be a base rate of 4 percent. If the price is above a certain level, then the rate jumps to 5 percent.

Hit another level and it goes to 6 percent, then 7 percent, perhaps all the way to 10 percent.

If you're a seller, you may be thinking that you like the low base rate, but not the later rates because they are too high. Keep in mind that by the time that agent qualifies for a 10 percent rate, the price will be so much higher that you will make much more money yourself.

Say you have a custom home in an area of homes with widely different designs and sizes. Since each home in the area is significantly different from all the others, they go for a wide range of prices. Averaging out the comps as best you can, you find that homes like yours have gone for prices ranging from a low of $300,000 to a high of $500,000. You would really love to sell it for $500,000. Yet you also know that if buyers just don't like your house, you might only be able to get $300,000. There is a $200,000 range of possible prices, depending on how buyers see your home.

Although the presentation of your home and market conditions are important, the agent's persuasiveness with a buyer can also make a big difference. To help get the highest price, you could suggest the following commission rate structure to your agent:

$350,000 or less = 4%
$350,000 to $450,0000 = 5
$450,000 to $500,000 = 6
Over $500,000 = 7

If the buyer is only willing to pay $350,000 or less, far below what you think the property is worth, the minimum commission rate of 4 percent will be all that the agent makes.

On the other hand, if the agent comes up with a buyer who pays $50,000 more, the commission will be 5 percent. A buyer who'll pay $100,000 more than that means an additional 6 percent. The bump-up continues until, should a buyer pay $550,000, the agent will earn 7 percent. The scale works out like this:

$$\$350,000 = \$14,000$$
$$\$400,000 = 22,500$$
$$\$500,000 = 30,000$$
$$\$550,000 = 38,500$$

Yes, it can work to your disadvantage. For example, if an agent sells the home for $449,000 you only owe a 5 percent commission. But, if the sales price is $450,100 you owe a 6 percent commission. Suddenly you're paying an extra (in this case) $4,500 when the price only goes up by a few hundred dollars. On the other hand, you're getting $100,000 more than the previous trigger point (at $350,000). You have to decide if it's more important to sell for a much higher price, or if it's more important to not pay the agent a bigger commission. (An alternative to this is to structure the commission bump-ups in terms of bonuses and not straight percentages—see following.)

In this fashion, the agent shares in the profitability of the home. The more a buyer pays for it, the bigger the rate of commission. The incentive is very strong to bring in high-price buyers.

Range Pricing

A few words of explanation are in order to show how a multirate listing would work and in what kind of market.

It may be possible to list your property for a price range depending on your state's listing rules and common practice. In some areas of the country, such as Southern California, it is not uncommon. In this arrangement, there isn't a single price for the home being listed. Instead, there is a range in the asking price—in this case from a low of $300,000 to a high over $500,000.

In actual practice, such a broad range is unlikely. Although a $200,000 range might be possible in a high-priced category, typically the range might be from $350,000 to $450,000, or even narrower. And the seller might start with a higher base commission and work up more quickly to a higher top rate.

Also, multirate pricing works best when the market is strong. In a weak market, there are lots of bottom-feeders—investors who are looking to pick up cheap properties—and you'll get many offers at the very bottom (or lower) end of your range.

Further, this works best in areas of custom or high-priced homes. If your home is in a tract where each house is pretty much like another, multirate commissions, as described here, probably won't work. There simply wouldn't be a big enough range for them. Every property's value would be clearly defined by recent comparable sales. However, a different version might work very well—a commission bonus.

The Commission Bonus

This variety of multirate commissioning works better in tract areas, where home prices are usually defined. Say you own a house in a tract and over the past year, prices for homes similar to yours have varied from a low of around $285,000 to a high of about $315,000. Thus, the average price is close to $300,000 with a 10 percent range (5 percent above to 5 percent below). Of course, you want $315,000, the top of the range.

One way to help get it is to be sure your home shows well. That includes landscaping and repainting the front, cleaning the carpets and painting inside, and fixing up kitchens and baths (see Appendixes A and B). There are many books on the market that show how to prepare a house for maximum effect on buyers (see my book, *Improve the Value of Your Home Up to $100,000*, New York: John Wiley & Sons, 2002).

Another way is to offer a bonus to the agent who brings in a buyer for top dollar. The bonus has three conditions:

Bonus Conditions

1. It goes *only* to the selling office. The listing office does not share in it (unless it is also the selling office).
2. It is based on the sales price.
3. It includes a lower rate of commission.

Say that in your area the typical commission is around 6 percent. Instead of paying the full 6 percent, you offer 5 or even 4 percent, plus a bonus of 20 percent. Range pricing may be used. If it is, the house would be listed between $285,000 and $315,000. If not, it would be listed for a straight $315,000. The bonus would be paid for each dollar over the minimum ($285,000) that a buyer paid. At a rate of 20 percent, the bonus comes to an extra $200 for each $1,000 more the buyer pays:

Bonus

$285,000 = 11,400 @ 4%
290,000 = 1,000 more
300,000 = 3,000 more
310,000 = 5,000 more
315,000 = 6,000 more

For the agent who produces buyers, the incentive is high because this bonus is not going to be shared with the listing office. It only goes to the selling office (unless an agent in the listing office finds the buyer).

For you, it works out very well, too. If you only end up getting minimum price for your house, you pay a minimum commission of 4 percent of $285,000 or $11,400. At the average price of $300,000, you're paying a $3,000 bonus on top of a $12,000 commission (@ 4 percent rate) or $15,400. This is well below the $18,000 you'd owe on a straight 6 percent commission.

At the top price of $315,000, you'd be paying $18,500 (assuming a base commission rate of 4 percent plus a $6,000 bonus), roughly what you'd pay on a straight 6 percent commission. But, you'd be selling at the top of the range for your home.

The idea here is that you pay top dollar on the commission only when you get top price for your home. Because of the bonus structure, you pay a lower commission (base rate plus bonus) for a lower price. The incentive then is to bring in the highest possible offer.

8

Basing the Commission on the Speed of Sale

The old stereotype about selling a house is that you list and wait . . . and wait . . . and wait. Except in very hot markets (which we've had for the past few years), it may take take weeks, months—sometimes a year or more—to find a buyer who wants to purchase just your property out of all the other hundreds (thousands) of properties for sale in your area.

Often sellers do not have a lot of time to sell a home. They may have a job opportunity in another state. There could be a divorce, and the property needs to be divided. There may be an urgent need for the money from the house to pay for medical expenses, college tuition, or some other emergency. For whatever reason, the sellers need a quick sale. Fast. Now!

How do they get it? Here are some novel ideas it's unlikely your average agent will have heard of. Consider them experiments you may want to try.

Selling for Investment Value

One sure way to get a quick sale is to repeatedly drop the price. Many relocation firms and investors use this technique. For example, they may drop the price of the property $5,000 a week. For the first week, the home is listed at full price, say $200,000. The second week, the price drops to $195,000. The third week, it drops to $190,000. The fourth week, it goes down to $185,000. And so on.

This only works if there is a major effort to get the word out. Real estate agents should receive flyers, e-mails, faxes, and phone calls informing them what's happening. They, in turn, contact buyers who have been waiting for good deals, usually investors. Then it becomes a game of who is going to jump first.

Investors typically spot this property and hover around it watching each other and waiting for the price to drop so low that it's a "steal" that no one can afford to let go by. When the right moment comes, the lucky investor moves quickly so as not to lose out.

Typically by the third or fourth week, there's an offer—sometimes more than one—and the house sells, probably for below its true market value (which could have been achieved by waiting for a buyer who wanted to move into it). In seeking a quick sale, the sellers accepted less than the property could have produced by waiting. They sold it for the home's "investment" value instead of its "habitat" value.

I'm not suggesting that you offer your home at "fire sale" prices to get out. You surely won't want to sacrifice your profit. If you're heavily financed, you may not even be able to sell in this fashion because you owe too much. I'm merely pointing out that selling for your home's investment value (as opposed to its habitat value) is a sure way to quickly move any home in any market.

Spurring Agent Interest

Another, and perhaps better, way of selling your home quickly, but for more money, is to give agents an incentive to work on it. There are probably hundreds, perhaps thousands of agents, in your community. Each of these agents comes in contact with many real buyers every week. Of course, these agents are trying to find just the right home for each buyer. But, if they are aware of a particular house, they are likely to bring it up and show it. And by just playing the numbers, the more talked up your home is, the more often it's shown, the more likely it is to get sold.

So, the question becomes how to spur your agent's interest in selling your home quickly. One method is the time-related bonus, as opposed to the price-related bonus discussed in the previous chapter. It is seldom used, but may work well, depending on your situation, and how daring you are.

The Time-Related Bonus

Here you offer a bonus to the selling agent (not to the listing agent). The sooner the sale is made, the higher the bonus. Here's a typical time-related bonus structure:

Time-Related Bonus

Week 1	$5,000
Week 2	4,000
Week 3	3,000
Week 4	2,000
Week 5	1,000
Week 6	–0–

The sooner an agent brings in a buyer, the larger the bonus. This should produce a frenzy of activity in the first couple of weeks and, hopefully, a buyer. After a few weeks, as the reward goes down, the activity will taper off if the home still hasn't sold. Even after 6 weeks, when there's no longer any bonus, there's a residual benefit because so many agents have heard of, seen, and shown your home. With all this publicity, it might sell in 8 weeks, as opposed to 4 months, and you would not have to pay any bonus.

With a bonus, you have to carefully consider the price and the commission. Although it is tempting to list the home for a higher price (because you're paying a bonus for a buyer), that's not likely to produce results. Remember, you're giving agents an incentive here, not buyers. There's no bonus to the buyers, so why should they pay more than the house is worth?

On the other hand, homes have a range of prices for which they can sell. The range for your home may be between $210,000 and $195,000. With the bonus, you might wisely choose to list at the top end ($210,000) of the range. If you get the top price, then even with the bonus you will have saved money (over selling at the lower end of the range without a bonus).

Adjusting the Commission to the Bonus

There's also the matter of the commission. If you're offering a bonus, then you might feel comfortable reducing the commission. Say a house similar to yours sells for $200,000 at a straight 6 percent commission after being listed four months. Instead, you list your house at 4 percent with a $4,000 bonus, and it sells after one week for $205,000.

The other sellers paid a $12,000 commission, but waited 4 months for a sale. You also paid a total of $12,000 commission, but sold within a week and made an extra $5,000 on the sale. Who came out better?

Your home may have taken more than a week to sell (in which case the bonus would have gone down), and it might not have sold for more than the other house. But even so, chances are you would have gotten a much quicker sale.

It's important to note that the bonus goes to the selling office. If you list for a 4 percent commission, that typically breaks down to 1 percent for the listing office and 3 percent for the selling office. In other words, the selling office is still getting a full selling commission (½ of 6 percent) plus the bonus. For selling agents, your house is a gold mine, a bonanza. You should see all kinds of action. And the selling office is likely to participate as well, hoping to come up with a buyer and thereby collect the full commission and the bonus.

––––––––––

Note: For our example, we're using a $4,000 to $5,000 bonus. That's rather high on a $200,000 house. You might want the bonus to be $3,000 or $2,000, or more or less, depending on the price of your home, the condition of the market, and how desperate you are to get out quickly.

Using a Commission Structure Tied to Time

It is possible to tie the agent's commission to the speed of the sale:

Time-Related Commission

1 month	7%	Split 50/50
2 months	6%	Split 50/50
3 months	5%	3% to selling office
4 months	4%	3% to selling office

Here the rate of commission is tied to the amount of time it takes to sell the property. If the house sells within the first month, the commission is high (7 percent). If it takes two months, a lower 6 percent commission is paid. After three months, it drops down to 5 percent, and so on.

Note that the selling office's share never gets below 3 percent, meaning that selling agents should have an incentive to find you a buyer. The listing agent's split, however, deteriorates over time, meaning they will want to hustle, at least initially, to get the higher commission.

The advantage of this system is that you're likely to get a frenzy of activity from the listing office and from would-be selling offices in the first month or so. Everyone will be running around trying to find a buyer to collect the higher commission.

As time goes by, however, and the commission rate drops, so will the activity on your home, at least from your lister. There will be some residual effect, but it is likely to be dampened by a falling commission schedule.

Listing at the high end of the price for your home amplifies this pattern. At the beginning of the listing period, you'll have a top-of-the-range price home but also a high commission rate, which should tend to balance each other out. If it sells within a week, you'll owe a bigger commission but probably you'll also have sold for a higher price. If the home still hasn't sold by the third month, you'll have a high price but a low commission rate, which could be the kiss of death in finding a buyer.

Therefore, if the home doesn't sell quickly, you'll need to reduce the price to lower in the range for your home to make it more attractive to buyers.

If you decide to tie the commission to time, limit the listing to no more than 3 months. If the home hasn't sold by then, relist either with a new agent or the same one, but use a different plan.

Setting the Listing Price

Any of these methods can produce lowball offers that are far below your asking price. Typically, they come from investors, but also sometimes from habitat buyers, who are looking for a bargain. They realize you need to get out quickly and, consequently, hope you will take a low price.

From your perspective, the last thing you want to do is to pay some sort of time bonus and then have to accept a lowball price. The whole point is to get both a quick sale and a good price. You're not obliged to take any offer below the asking price for which you've listed your home. If you list for $210,000 and an offer comes in for $180,000, you don't need to accept it no matter how much you're pressured, and no commission or bonus is due. (Be sure to have your attorney review your listing agreement.)

Indeed, even if an offer comes in for full price or above, you're not obligated to sell. However, you may be obligated to pay a commission and a bonus. Again, have your attorney check the listing. If it states that the agent is entitled to a commission on producing a buyer who is "ready, willing, and able" to purchase at your listed price and under your listed terms, you may very well owe a commission. On the other hand, if a commission and bonus are to be paid only on an actual sale (close of escrow), you may not owe the agent any money should you refuse to sell.

Alternatives to Selling

Thus far, we've considered sellers who must sell quickly to get the money out of the property. However, there are ways of avoiding such pressure. You may be able to refinance and rent out your home, thus avoiding the possibilities of a slow sale, a low price, and a big commission. Sellers today can more easily refinance their home and pull money out. (This was not possible only a decade ago.) If your home falls under the heading of a "conforming" loan, there are myriad refinancing possibilities.

Conforming means that it conforms to the underwriting guidelines of Fannie Mae and Freddie Mac. These are the two huge secondary lenders who buy mortgages from the lending institutions that originate these loans. The following underwriting guidelines are the most crucial:

- Mortgage is within maximum amount, currently $327,700.
- Owner occupies the property. (Loan amounts are lower and interest rates may be higher for absentee owners/landlords.)
- Owner has good credit, usually exhibited as a credit score (FICO) of around 660 or higher.

- Owner has sufficient income in the eyes of the lender to make payments.

Note: You must intend to occupy the property. So get this financing while you're still in the house, long before you intend to switch your property to a rental.

If you qualify under these guidelines, you may be able to get financing for up to 100 percent of your home's value and pull much or all of your equity out. Check with a good mortgage broker.

The idea here is to pull as much of your equity as possible out of your home. Then, later on, you can rent it to cover your costs of mortgage, taxes, insurance, and maintenance and repair. You take the money and go on your way or spend it as needed. In real life, renting out property for enough to cover all the costs is rarely possible. Because the rental income does not cover all expenses, the owner gets into a negative cash flow situation. Before embarking on this course, thoroughly investigate not only how much financing you can get, but also how much rent you can reasonably expect to collect on your house (including rent-up and move-out times).

There are many books on the market that can help you make this decision (see Robert Irwin, *Buy, Rent, and Sell,* New York: McGraw-Hill, 2001).

Renting out your home as an alternative to selling and paying a hefty commission may not be your cup of tea. But, for some it's the perfect answer.

Creating Your
Own Listing
Agreement

Why in the world would you, as the seller, want your own listing agreement? Isn't this something the agent normally provides?

Yes, that's usually the way it works, but the purpose of this book is to explore listing structures that are often far afield from the usual arrangement. All agents are ready to pop up with an "Exclusive Right to Sell" agreement for you to sign. But, what if that's not the agreement that you want? What if you want a net listing or a commission based on the speed of sale, or would like a bonus tied to the price? How do you come up with the appropriate listing for these variations?

Your agent will probably want to modify the standard listing agreement. You'll just cross out this, add that, initial here and there, and voilà, a new listing agreement has been created just for your needs.

Will this work?

Maybe. But, just as a purchase agreement ties buyer and seller together and is intended to be a legally binding document, the terms in the listing agreement legally bind the seller and the listing office. And unless it spells out exactly what you have in mind, when it comes time to pay the commission, fee, or bonus, you could be unpleasantly surprised.

Therefore, if you're doing a creative listing, you need to come up with a creative listing agreement.

Getting Past, "It's Our Policy"

One of the big arguments that an agent may offer against diverging from the standard commission rate listing is that there is no way physically to deal with it. The listing agreement is only written one way. The agent may even say, "It's our policy to only work with our own listing agreements."

How do you deal with the roadblock that an "our policy" statement places in your path?

The answer is that after you explain again what you want, either the agent will get out from behind the cover of the statement, or you'll have to find another agent. Some real estate people work on the cookbook principle. If the recipe is in the cookbook, they can make it (list it). If it's not in the cookbook, they simply can't handle it. Thus, whether you come in with strange ingredients or want an unusual structure for paying the commission, your agent either works by the cookbook or can be creative. You'll quickly discover which it is.

Note: Some agents may say that their broker/franchise company will not accept anything other than their standard listing. This may very well be true, in which case you'll have to politely excuse them and look for either an independent broker or a franchise company that is more creative in taking listings.

Work with Your Agent

Once you find an agent who's willing to work with you on a new and different kind of commission structure, you must come up with a written document. An agent who is used to working with a specific listing agreement is not going to be thrilled to learn that on top of coming up with a new commission structure, you also want a new listing agreement. You can point out that it is to your mutual advantage. You don't want to pay more than agreed on, and your agent doesn't want you to pay any less. Therefore, the best policy is to work together to come up with an equitable arrangement and then have your attorney finalize it.

There are two steps here. In the first step, you and your agent negotiate the terms of the listing agreement, as discussed in the previous chapters. You decide exactly what kind of listing you want and the specific terms under which you'll pay the agent.

The second step is to have an attorney finalize this arrangement in a legal document. How can an agent object to this procedure?

Note: Because it will require more time to create the listing from scratch, let your attorney work with and modify the agent's standard listing agreement. This will help put your agent at ease and will make your attorney's job easier. And, it will probably reduce the legal fee.

Understanding Listing Agreements

The various standard listing agreements are discussed in the remainder of this chapter. Your agent undoubtedly is familiar with, or at least has heard of, all these formats. You need to decide which one comes closest to fitting your needs and then have your attorney modify it. (Your agent and your attorney may be able to help with suggestions.)

Standard Real Estate Listing Agreements
Open Listing
Here you are giving any interested agent the right to sell your property. You are opening up your property to all agents, and no

one agent or agency can claim exclusive rights to your listing, as illustrated in the following example.

You give an open listing to Pauline of MNO Realty. Your listing says that if Pauline brings in a buyer who is ready, willing, and able to purchase and/or who ultimately buys your home, you'll pay Pauline a commission as described. The commission can take almost any form suggested in this book.

You give this listing not only to Pauline, but also to Paul and to every other agent who comes by your door. Under an open listing, you can list unlimited times with an unlimited number of agents. The reason is that you'll only pay a commission to that one agent who comes by and produces a buyer. As soon as that happens, all the other agents have no claim on you.

If that sounds great to you, it is. However, it's not so great for either Pauline or Paul. They may spend time, money, and effort to find a buyer for your property and then lose out to a different agent who brings in a buyer before them. Since they have no assurance that they will receive a commission, why should they expend any effort on your property?

In practice, they won't. While agents may very well accept an open listing, don't expect them to search for a buyer. As far as they are concerned, only if a buyer, desperate to purchase your property knocks on their door, will they answer.

Exclusive Agency Listing

This is an answer to the open listing that helps satisfy agents. It says that you've given this agent an exclusive on your property. Only Pauline, in this case, can collect a commission from you. You give this listing to just one agent and no others can collect that commission *from you.*

Does this mean that other agents can't work on the property? No, it doesn't. They can indeed work on the property, as long as Pauline lets them. Paul may have a buyer. So instead of calling you, he calls Pauline. She says, "Sure, bring the buyer by. I'll split the commission I get with you." (Usually, real estate boards or the offices involved have already established commission splits.) Of course, Paul is happy to work on your listing. Although only Pauline can act as your agent and collect a commission from you, Paul can collect part of Pauline's commission from her.

Once again, the way you pay the commission can be based on your negotiations with the agent.

If the exclusive agency listing sounds perfect for the agent, think again. From the agent's perspective, there's still a problem. What if, after spending considerable time, money, and effort, Pauline finally comes up with a qualified buyer and discovers that in the meantime, you've sold your property on your own to Larry over in the next county?

The exclusive agency listing protects Pauline from other agents undermining her and getting a commission from you. But, she's in no way protected from you. While she's out there trying to make a sale, you could be doing the same thing on your own. And because you know that if you find a buyer first, you won't have to pay a commission, you're working twice as hard as she is!

Further, what if she showed the house to a potential buyer who later comes by and offers to purchase it directly from you? Will you pay Pauline a commission? What if you never saw her bring the buyer by your home? What if you think she has made the whole thing up? What if the potential buyer insists that he never worked with Pauline? What if the buyer's lying hoping to get a better price from you?

To collect a commission, Pauline might have to institute a lawsuit against you proving that the purchaser was indeed her buyer. That might be difficult. And even if successful, she might have to absorb legal costs. Most agents won't work much harder on an exclusive agency listing than they will on an open listing because they fear that you'll find a buyer on your own or that you will get together with the agent's buyer behind the agent's back. It simply is not worth it.

Note: Agents sometimes solve this problem by asking for a restrictive listing. The agent who has a possible buyer for your home may come by and ask for a one-day listing to show your home to that party. The potential buyer's name will be revealed to you, and you'll have to sign an agreement stating that if the person does eventually purchase, you'll pay a commission.

Exclusive Right-to-Sell

The answer to the exclusive agency agreement, at least from the agent's perspective, is the exclusive right-to-sell. Here, you agree to pay Pauline a commission no matter who sells the property, even if it's you, the owner.

This arrangement means there can be no dispute about who showed the property to whom first. You and the would-be buyer can't reach an agreement behind Pauline's back to sell at a lower price, but avoid a commission. Even if you sell the property, you still owe a commission. It is not surprising that the standard listing that most agents prefer is the exclusive right-to-sell agreement. It gives them the most protection and the most reason to spend time, money, and effort in selling your property. From the agent's perspective, it's perfect.

Almost any payment structure you decide on can usually be placed under an exclusive right-to-sell.

Note: Most exclusive right-to-sell listings have a time extension specifying that if you sell to anybody who first saw the property through the agent you may still owe the agent a commission. This requirement applies if the sale occurs within 60 days (sometimes 30 or 90) after the listing has expired. The purpose is to prevent a buyer from colluding with you to avoid a commission, usually near the end of a listing.

Net Listing

This listing can be an element in any one of the three listings previously described; it refers specifically to the payment arrangement. As described in Chapter 7, in a net listing you set a price for your property. If it sells below that price, the agent gets nothing. If it sells for more than the stated price, the agent gets the entire excess amount. All you're concerned with is netting a certain fixed sum of money.

Say you want to sell your home for $275,000, net. That's the amount that you receive (not counting the payoff on your financing and the usual closing costs). Were you to list this for a 6 percent commission, you'd probably want to list it for around $292,500. If the property sold for this amount, your net would be roughly $275,000 after paying the 6 percent commission.

In this example, we didn't consider the market value of your property. If its market value was only around $275,000, then your chances of netting that much would be nil. On the other hand, if its value was higher, then your chances would be excellent. And on a net listing, the higher the amount over your net, the more the agent gets. If the property actually sells for $300,000, then the agent gets $25,000, a handsome amount.

If you intend to use a net listing, be sure that you have an excellent idea of your property's true market value. Otherwise, you could lose money on this transaction. (Also, be sure to check out the other pitfalls of a net listing described in Chapter 7.)

Know What "Ready, Willing, and Able" Means

Most listing agreements still include a phrase stating that you owe a commission when the agent produces a buyer who is *ready, willing, and able* to purchase. Note, this does not say that you owe the commission when the buyer actually purchases and the sale goes through. You owe the commission when the buyer meets the specified qualifications even if no sale takes place.

Don't think this can't occur. You list your home and then, for whatever reason (change of employment, financial crisis, divorce, rise in home prices, and so on), you decide not to sell. But, during the listing period, your agent produces a buyer who is ready, willing, and able for the terms and price listed.

Do you have to sell? No.

Do you have to pay a commission? Probably!

To avoid this problem, some sellers have started amending the listing agreement to state that the commission isn't payable until the escrow actually closes. That way, no sale, no commission owed.

If you want to have this safeguard, be sure to check with your attorney.

Nine Strategies
for Helping
Your Agent

Never lose track of your goal, which is to sell your home. Yes, you want to save money on the transaction costs, mainly the commission, but even if you get a broker to work for 1 percent commission and your home never sells, what good is it?

To sell your home, at least two different agents need to work hard—the lister and the buyer's agent. (Sometimes, of course, they are one and the same.) Don't downplay the importance of either.

The listing broker can be critical to selling your property. A different agent may bring in a buyer, but without the solid efforts of your listing broker, that other agent might never have heard about your house, might never have shown it, and might never have written up a purchase agreement.

That selling agent needs to find your home attractive, both physically and financially. Your lister can only go so far: After that, it's up to the house to sell itself.

Thus, a smart seller will make every effort to encourage the efforts of both the lister and the buyer's agents. Your helpfulness may mean the difference between a quick sale and one that takes month, a sale for a good price, or no sale at all.

This chapter describes nine ways you can help your agent (use these strategies *after* you've agreed on the commission structure—see earlier chapters).

Strategy 1. Use Cash Bonuses Wisely

Everyone likes a bonus and real estate agents are no exception. Money talks and bonuses speak directly. The key to the money bonus is to tie it to a specific performance that you're seeking. As discussed in Chapter 7, it can be tied to price. Or it can be tied to time, as described in Chapter 8. Or it can simply be tied to finding a buyer as in, "I'll pay a $500 [or $1,000 or whatever] bonus to any agent who brings me a buyer." In all these cases, the bonus is aimed squarely at the agent who brings in the buyer.

On the other hand, it also can be tied to the listing agent's performance. If your agent gives you a lot of open houses, caravans, and publicity, why not reward that effort with a bonus? This is on top of the commission and may *or may not* be tied to a sale.

Note: You should set up the bonus early in the sales effort to encourage superior performance by the agent; it serves no purpose as an afterthought.

The whole idea of the bonus is to encourage good work. You want to be sure you don't give out a bonus for poor performance. Supposing your home languishes on the market for months with nary an agent, let alone a buyer, coming to see it. Finally, someone drops by because of the sign in front and you talk the person into buying. You owe the agent a commission because you've signed an exclusive right-to-sell listing (see Chapter 9). But should you pay a bonus? I certainly hope not!

A bonus can be particularly effective if you're offering a relatively low commission rate. It can sometimes buy you enthusiasm while saving you money overall.

Caution: You cannot pay a bonus directly to the selling salesperson. As explained in Chapter 2, commissions (including bonuses) can only go to a licensed broker. The broker can then pay a portion of the bonus to the salesperson working under the broker's license.

_____

Thus, when you say you'll pay the bonus or the commission, ". . . to the selling agent," what you're really saying is that it goes to the selling office.

Strategy 2. Consider Awards

This sometimes works as well as, or even better than, cash. With a cash bonus, the salesperson who brings in the buyer gets a percentage split of the bonus (part goes to the broker). But, what if instead of a cash bonus, you're giving away a brand-new 36-inch Sony television set?

It still goes to the selling agent's office. But how do you split a TV? The broker may be a real tightwad and demand a few hundred dollars in cash from the selling agent. But in most offices, the entire TV will go to the listing agent who worked hard. Thus, awards can often be better incentives than cash.

Of course, you are not limited by television sets. And you're not limited to giving them to the listing agent. You can give them to the buyer's agent as well. There's no limit to the imagination when it comes to awards. Some of the best incentives are vacations. (The agent who produces a buyer gets an all-expense-paid vacation to Hawaii for a week!)

Too expensive for you? Once you look into awards, you may be surprised to find that vacation deals are all over the place. The major airlines often offer incredibly cheap round-trip airfares, and "all expenses" usually means just hotel and travel with, perhaps, a few meals. It can be done for one or two thousand dollars.

It doesn't have to be Hawaii. What about Las Vegas? Or Mexico? Or even Disney World?

I once knew a seller who was very clever in choosing an award. He had a seven-year-old Lexus that was in terrific shape. Since he was buying a new car, he offered the Lexus as an award to the agent who produced the buyer.

If you don't think agents scrambled to find buyers, you are sadly mistaken. The car may have been a used vehicle, but it was in great shape. And it was a Lexus! The owner was selling a home in the $550,000 price range, so the car's value (around $8,000) was something he felt he could afford—and still make money on the deal.

An award, like a bonus, can result in a better price, a quicker sale, or both. Combined with a reduced commission rate, it can save you thousands.

Strategy 3. Try Merit Prizes

The listing agent is a vital partner in the sales effort. To get a sale, it's critical for your listing agent to let other agents know the property is out there. The agent who simply lists and puts a sign in front of your house is only letting your neighbors know it is for sale. The agent who gets the word out to all the other brokers is engaging a huge selling machine.

To get your agent to make an extra effort, you can offer small prizes for work well done, even if no sale is immediately realized. For example, there are the caravans noted earlier. A single caravan usually is scheduled when the agent first lists the property. But caravans can be organized again, sometimes every few weeks, especially for other real estate offices. I know an agent who gets the homes she lists on at least three caravans the first month of the listing.

Your agent's broker may have many offices in the area. And sometimes competing offices also participate. The listing salesperson makes certain that your home is on the list of houses for caravans with agents who haven't seen it before. My suggestion is that you pay the agent for caravans, particularly after the first one.

Whoopee! So you give your listing agent $100 or $200 for every caravan that includes your house. You may say to yourself, what possible good can come from 25 or 50 or even 100 agents spending a total of 2 minutes each looking at your home? How can that possibly inspire them to find a buyer?

The easiest way to explain this is to think of a person who sells a technical product, say digital cameras. Kathy sells them for a major electronics store day in and day out. If you come by, it might take her 10 minutes just to explain what a digital camera is. It could take half a day for you to become slightly familiar with half a dozen models.

Kathy sometimes visits other electronic stores to see what they are offering. She rarely spends more than a few minutes looking at the digital camera display. During that time, she identifies every model they have, knows what those models offer, and looks at the prices. She also checks out the attractiveness of the display and notices how customers are responding to it. Kathy is a pro in her field. It takes her only minutes to absorb what would take us hours.

The same holds true for real estate professionals. They may whiz in and out of your house, but during that brief visit they have probably noted everything that is important. Oh, perhaps they may overlook the door to an attic you've renovated unless you point it out. But as far as the major features, the size, the layout, the condition, the location—you can bet they've got it all. (That's what comes from looking at dozens of houses every week.)

Therefore, you want to encourage your listing agent to put your house on a caravan's schedule. If you've arranged a discount commission, however, your agent may be unenthusiastic about making the extra effort unless you offer a bonus, say a couple of hundred dollars, or an award of some sort.

In many cases, a reduced commission means it's reduced only for the selling agent. That might cause an agent to sit back and do nothing. Giving a merit award for arranging a caravan or for calling, faxing, and e-mailing or otherwise promoting your property could be just what it takes to get your agent moving.

Strategy 4. Encourage Agents-Only Open Houses

Listing agents are usually happy to hold an open house for you. They'll advertise it in the paper, put out flyers and signs, and sit there all afternoon on a Sunday waiting for prospects to come by. As noted, this does you little good. Buyers' open houses are simply a great device for the agent to attract new clients, both sellers and buyers. Few people who come to an open house end up buying the property.

On the other hand, you can count on many of your neighbors coming by. They want to see the inside of your home. They want to compare it with theirs and speculate how much their home is worth if you're asking such and such. Buyers for other homes will also come by because many of them have their own homes to sell.

Does any of this help you?

Hardly! But, it allows the agent to meet your neighbors and talk with them. Your agent can talk with them and find out who's thinking about selling in the near future. And, an agent who is good at it can pick up another listing from your open house. Or perhaps a buyer for another house. I watched as a hot agent talked to a wannabe buyer who stopped at an open house, then quickly locked up the house, and drove that buyer to another house on which they wrote up a deal!

Your open house is a great opportunity for your agent to find buyers with whom to work. That's why agents are so eager to hold open houses. But, this rarely benefits you directly. (It benefits you indirectly in that an agent holding an open house elsewhere may have seen your house while caravaning and may bring a buyer from that open house over to see yours . . . and sell it.)

Holding an *agents-only* open house, is a totally different story. Here, agents are encouraged to come by and see your home. As with caravans, the agents' visits are brief, just in and out. But, once they've seen your home, they'll tend to remember it and show it to buyers.

So, you want to encourage your agent to hold an agents-only open house. How do you do this? By helping with the cost.

Agents are typically loath to put up any front money. Agents working on a discount commission are doubly loath to do so. The reason is that any money the agent puts up, even a small amount, may never yield a return if your home doesn't sell. Agents don't get paid (usually) unless there's a sale. No sale, no pay. It's one thing if the agent is only out time and effort on your behalf (plus the usual costs of doing business such as car, office, phone, and so on). But, it's something else if the agent has out-of-pocket expenses specifically for your home.

You may be saying, it's an investment in the agent's business. Yes, it is. But until you've been in the agent's position of having to cover extra costs in the hope that a house might sell, don't be too critical. Many houses simply don't sell. And if the agent were to foot the bill personally of promoting every home, that agent might not survive long in the business. (As it is, agents usually pay for standard costs such as putting a sign in front, listing your home on the Multiple Listing Service (MLS), and doing some advertising.)

Offering to foot the bill will encourage an agent to hold an agents-only open house (especially an agent who is already receiving a discounted commission).

Provide champagne, coffee, and snacks (appetizers, cookies, and so on). If your agent spreads the word that you are hosting a champagne open house just for people in the business, they'll come. Chances are they'll come in droves. And that will go a long way toward promoting your property and getting it sold.

(If your home doesn't sell within a month, sponsor a second agents-only open house . . . and later even a third.)

Strategy 5. Keep in Close Contact

I firmly believe in the old adage: "The squeaky wheel gets the oil." Sellers who never call the agent are likely to be categorized as passive or complacent. These sellers are satisfied whether the house takes 1 week to sell or 9 weeks. They don't complain about the lack of traffic (few wannabe buyers coming through). They never make a fuss. These sellers will let anyone, including their agent, walk all over them. Are you this kind of seller?

I hope not. On the other hand, I also hope you're not the kind of seller who calls the agent daily, stops by the agent's office every other day, and writes the agent e-mails every 3 hours.

This seller is such a pest that the agent is likely to simply turn off and tune out, if not give the listing back.

You want to be persistent, but not a nuisance. You want to take action, but not be constantly in your agent's face. You want to be helpful, but not aggravating. For some of us, this is not an easy line to walk. It can be difficult to keep close contact with your agent without overdoing it. Neither do you want to simply let things go for weeks and months on end.

Ultimately, you'll have to strike a balance. Calling an agent at least once a week is a good idea. You can find out what promotions your agent has undertaken that week and whom the agent has contacted (get a list of names of other agents), which buyers were interested, what advertising has been done, what e-mails, faxes, and so on have been sent. It's not unreasonable to request such information. After all, you want your agent to be actively at work. And active agents are usually happy to point out all the work they have done.

It is okay to call an agent any reasonable time of the day to ask a specific question or to give the agent a lead. This does not mean calling every afternoon to question the agent's progress.

It is also acceptable to stop by the agent's office occasionally (every couple of weeks or so) to chat with other agents in the office to see if your agent has, indeed, talked up your property, and to get to know the broker.

Keeping in contact with your agent will demonstrate that you're anxious to get your property sold and also will send a message that you're not going to be happy with inactivity on the agent's part. At the same time, it doesn't identify you as a "nervous Nelly" who needs reassurance daily.

Keep in contact. But don't overdo it.

Strategy 6. Offer to Pay for Little Things

A good listing agent will pay for the essentials, such as listing the property on the MLS and putting out a sign, even if the commission is discounted. But, the agent pays for a lot of little things that might get lost in the shuffle of a discount deal:

- Flyers describing your home
- Small but effective (3-line) advertisements in the news-paper
- Fax calls (each call can cost something)
- Website featuring your home
- Transportation (gas, wear and tear on car) going to see other agents, showing your home, and so on

All these expenses together might not cost a hundred dollars or so a month. But, an agent who is already getting a reduced commission, might question putting out that extra money.

So why not offer to pay for it yourself? It won't cost you much, but you'll come across as someone who understands the problems of being a real estate agent and who cares about the person beyond the agent. A few hundred dollars properly spent can earn you a world of gratitude and action.

Strategy 7. Help with Phone Calls

Selling a home often involves "cold calling." This is usually the bane of salespeople. In fact, I've rarely met a salesperson who would admit to enjoying this task. In real estate, it means dropping by to ask people in the neighborhood if they know of someone who might want to buy your home (such as themselves).

For an agent, this can mean not only finding a buyer for your home, but finding potential buyers and sellers for other properties. Hence, agents grin and bear it. Sometimes.

For you, on the other hand, it simply means calling up your friendly neighbors (even ones you haven't spoken to in years) and letting them know your property is for sale, telling them the price, and inviting them to come by and see it. And, "by the way," giving them the name and phone number of your agent in case they know someone who wants to buy it.

All that has to happen is for one neighbor to call your agent and express interest in buying your property or furnish a lead to someone who might be selling a home, and your agent will be energized. You will become a heroine (or hero). The agent will put out 110 percent to sell your property. After all, you're going out and finding them clients!

Since you're neighbors, you can simply strike up a conversation. I've sold homes to friends and relatives of neighbors. Who knows where a few words will lead?

Note: Be careful whom you call—calling for solicitation has been restricted or outlawed.

Strategy 8. Do Your Own Promotion

There's also nothing to prevent you from sending out flyers, faxes, and e-mails to other agents, friends, associates, and anyone who might even be remotely interested in your home. You can even put up your own website and take out your own ads without offending your agent provided you've signed an exclusive-right-to-sell listing. As noted, with this listing you agree to pay a commission to your agent no matter who sells your home, even if it's you.

If you plan to do this, let your agent know—don't make it a surprise; coordinate with your agent. You can list your agent's number although many media do not allow ads to go to agents unless they are identified as such. Even if you give your own number, you can field calls and refer serious buyers to your agent.

Doing your own promotion will definitely cost you something in time and effort, and possibly a little money, but it can light a fire under an agent.

Strategy 9. Be Positive

Nobody likes a grouch. Even if things are going bad, you've had no offers, no wannabe buyers have come through, and no agents have been looking, try to stay upbeat. Look to the future for progress instead of to the past for blame. This is not to say you should let an inactive agent off the hook. You should be firm and demanding. But never yell, get physically aggressive, or threatening. Remember, your agent not only works for you, but should be a friend. You want to be on good terms with your agent so that you can call at any time and get a ready response.

If you act like a jerk, you'll simply get your agent to turn you off and spread your reputation to other agents. That will almost certainly slow down the sale of your home and even, potentially, result in lower offers.

It's simple. Be nice. It costs nothing, and it's great advice in life as well as in real estate.

11

Paying Just for Services Performed

Remember the old story about a guy who decided to build a car piece by piece instead of buying one ready to go? He figured he could save money if he bought the frame, engine, transmission, and all the other parts and put them together himself. When he was finished, however, he discovered that he had paid three times more than it would have cost to buy the car fully assembled.

The moral of this story is that when you buy a car, you should get one that is completely assembled. In real estate, however, the same approach is not always advisable. Sometimes when you're selling your home, you can save thousands of dollars by purchasing just the parts, or assistance, that you need.

You may want to sell your home on your own, or you may want to do part of the work yourself and consign the rest of it to professionals. In this chapter, we look at the latter arrangement.

Get an Attorney to Help

If you can come up with the buyer yourself, you can sometimes save a bundle by having an attorney do the paperwork. In some areas of the country, primarily the East Coast, this can be an easy solution because lawyers commonly handle much of the work of closing a real estate transaction. (In most of the rest of the country, escrow officers and real estate agents handle closings.)

Attorneys on the East Coast often handle the entire closing, including all the paperwork, for a flat fee, typically between $1,000 and $1,500 depending on the complexity of the closing and the price of the property. Since many attorneys charge more than $100 an hour for their regular services, the real estate fee has to be the best legal bargain on the planet.

For this fee, the attorney will also often put together the sales agreement, which is the document that binds seller to buyer and cements the deal.

Note: The attorney does not act as a salesperson for the buyer and seller. But, once a buyer has been found and the price and terms are agreed on, the lawyer will formalize the agreement in writing.

Finding a Buyer Yourself

The premise is that you can find a buyer and sell your home by yourself. Sometimes it is easy. A neighbor, friend, relative, associate, or other person who wants to buy finds out that you want to sell. What could be easier? Hire an attorney to handle the paperwork for a few thousand dollars and the deal is done— you've saved thousands of dollars.

Can you really do this . . . and save thousands?

It depends mostly on whether you are able to find a fee-for-service agent and can farm out only the services you don't want to handle by yourself.

What Is a Fee-for-Service Agent?

A "fee-for-service" agent is a licensed real estate agent operating a legitimate office who, instead of charging a commission based on the selling price, breaks down the sales transaction into its components and charges separately for each part. Just as you can buy the parts of a car separately, you can buy the parts of a real estate transaction.

The question immediately arises, isn't this more expensive than buying the whole car or the whole transaction?

That depends on the fee structure the agent uses and on how many services you need. Even if the fee structure is such that the sum of all fees is higher than a full commission, you may only need a few services. In that case, you could still save money over paying for a full-service agent.

Fee-for-service agents often have a price list similar to a restaurant menu. There may be a dozen or more separate items on it, each with a different price:

Agent's Price List

Sign (installed)	$100
Answering calls (per call)	25
Showing property (per showing)	200
Advertising (cost plus 10%)	??
Negotiating with buyer (per hour)	250
Listing (on the MLS)	750
Negotiating sales agreement	500
Dealing with disclosures	250
Analyzing inspection report	200
Scheduling inspections (per each)	100
Evaluating closing instructions	250
Attending closing	500

The preceding list is obviously not complete and the figures are not taken from any particular fee-for-service agent. However, they are similar to amounts you might come across. Do they seem inexpensive? Do they seem high? Since they are *not* tied to the sales price of the property, the pricier the home, the greater the bargain.

You can pick and choose services based on what you want and need. If you're going to get all the services and it takes lots of advertising, showings, and negotiations over a fairly long time to sell your home, it will cost more than if you had simply listed for a 6 percent commission, or even a flat rate.

On the other hand, if your home sells quickly or you do some of the work and hire an attorney to do some of it for you, you can save a considerable amount of money by hiring an agent on a fee basis.

Finding a Fee-for-Service Agent

This can be harder than it seems at first glance. A decade ago, fee-for-service agents were calling me from Virginia to California, from Texas to Oregon. They all wanted to be sure that I knew about and wrote up their services.

Many were start-up operations that used the Internet. Others were using big advertising campaigns through television and newspapers. Still others were operating simply by word of mouth. It was the hottest thing going.

Then, nothing. For the past few years, it has been difficult to find a fee-for-service agent in many areas. Some of those who started out so grandiosely couldn't make it and went out of business. Others made money, but not enough. And still others simply decided they didn't like doing business that way.

And then there was the liability. Many agents discovered that their liability was often the same whether they were getting a couple hundred dollars for showing the property or a full commission for making the whole deal. If the deal went bad and the seller or the buyer took legal action, they were as likely to get sued whether they had spent a month working on the deal for a full commission or had spent an hour and received $200.

And even if they were not found liable for anything, just the cost of defending themselves (including the premiums on the their errors and omissions insurance) was high.

These problems reduced the number of fee-for-service agents, but the pendulum seems to be swinging back. More agents are considering this approach, although their fee structure tends to be higher. And many will only work for a minimum amount, say several thousand dollars.

Thus, if you want to find a fee-for-service agent, you may have to hunt a bit. Here are some search techniques:

Finding a Fee-for-Service Agent

- *Recommendation.* This is usually one of the best methods. If a friend, associate, or relative has recently worked with a fee-for-service agent, ask for a recommendation and follow up on it. Nothing inspires confidence so much as a favorable testimonial from someone you know.
- *Other agents.* Agents may not be thrilled about recommending another agent. Carefully explain that you'd just like to investigate the possibility of using fee-for-service, and if things don't work out, you'll certainly reconsider full service. Many agents then will make a recommendation, if they know someone who is working on that basis.
- *Local real estate board.* Most agents belong to a real estate board, and someone at the board may know who works on a fee-for-service basis. The board may not want to discuss this because, among other reasons, it might appear to be recommending a particular payment structure, even if it is not a commission rate. However, it's probably worth a phone call.

- *Advertising.* Many fee-for-service agents advertise their services. You can find their ads in local newspapers (both daily and weekly) as well as in throwouts that come with your mail. Also check bulletin boards. Sometimes these agents also place small television or radio ads.
- *Internet.* Ads for fee-for-service agents may come as spam on the Internet. Otherwise, check out a good search engine such as Google. Use key words such as "fee-for-service real estate." But be sure that any Internet agent you have under consideration resides in your area, not somewhere across the country.
- *Yellow Pages.* As a last resort (and sometimes sooner), these directories usually identify fee-for-service agents in your area. These days, there are often two, three, or more yellow pages from different phone companies. You may need to check all of them to get a complete answer.

What if you try all the preceding suggestions and still can't find a fee-for-service agent in your area? In that case, work with full-service agents using one of the other plans discussed in this book. I do *not* recommend going out of your area and particularly not out of your state. Real estate sales are best handled by local agents who know the laws of their state as well as any idiosyncrasies of their immediate area.

Qualifying the Fee-for-Service Agent

Assuming that you find fee-for-service agents, spend enough time to qualify them. Make sure not only that they are enthusiastic, but that they also know what they are doing.

This is not to imply that agents working on a fee-for-service basis are any less knowledgeable or competent than other agents. However, a fee-for-service agent has given up the hope of a fat commission to accept, instead, a more regular but possibly lower hourly/daily/or weekly income. Try to make certain that the reason for this is not that the agent simply couldn't make it the other way. You want a terrific agent working for you regardless of the fee structure (also see Chapter 2).

Questions to Ask When Qualifying a Fee-for-Service Agent

• *How long have you been in the business?* The last thing you want is an agent who has just gotten a license and is dying to learn on you. Agents can't learn how to do a good job selling real estate simply by reading a book. And getting a license only means that they have memorized the basic real property laws of the state they live in. The only way agents learn is by making deals on the front lines. The more deals agents make, the more they learn about the different situations (crises) that come up and how to deal with them successfully. Look for at least 5 to 10 years' experience.

Try to find agents who used to work on regular commission basis and then switched to fee-for-service. Then ask them why they switched. A positive answer would be something like, "I make lots more money this way," or "I have less work to do and the stress is lower." You don't want to hear, "I just couldn't make it the other way and it was either switch or go out of business."

• *How active are you in the business?* This is another concern with fee-for-service agents. They may have been around for a long time but are inactive agents or part-timers. It might be that after they spent years coming into the office to read the paper, their broker simply kicked them out. Now, they're trying to generate some money on a fee-for-service basis to supplement retirement income from another source such as the military, education, or civil service.

This does not necessarily make them poor agents. Nevertheless, if there's another source of income and real estate is just a way to bring in a little extra, agents are less likely to be highly motivated to get out there and make deals. In fact, they probably haven't made many deals. So your next question should be:

• *How many deals have you made in the last 12 months?* The answer, as mentioned earlier in this book, should be 6 to 12. However, be wary of the agent who smiles and says something like, "Oh, I've been involved in at least 15 deals in the last year." "Been involved" covers a lot of territory. Ask the agent to be more specific. "Did you represent the sellers? The buyers? If not, in what way were you involved?" It may turn out that the agent simply sat in on some negotiations or answered a couple of questions for another agent. The true test is, did your subject agent get a commission on the deal? Without at least a partial commission of some sort or another, the agent didn't make a deal, no matter what the degree of involvement.

• *Do you belong to the local real estate board?* To belong to the board, the agent normally must be licensed and be a Realtor (a member of the National Association of Realtors, a trade group dedicated to promoting excellence in the field).

Belonging to the local board usually means that the agent can put your home on the MLS as well as cobroke with other agents. Not belonging to the local board might suggest a problem. If the agent doesn't belong, you should ask why. Was the person suspended or asked to leave? Did the agent have a legitimate disagreement with the board, or is there another reasonable explanation for the lack of membership?

Belonging to a local real estate board is not necessarily a requirement to be a successful agent. You have to wonder, however, why any agent would not want to belong to the largest trade organization in the real estate profession. Listen carefully to the agent's explanation.

• *Can you list my house on the MLS?* As noted, the agent usually must belong to the local real estate board to put your home on the MLS (although independent agents may make arrangements to place listings). Chances are that one of the services you will ask the agent to provide—often the most expensive one—is to list your home on the MLS so other agents will know about it and can work on it. If you want this service, be sure the agent can offer it to you.

• *Are you a broker or a salesperson?* A straight commissioned agent usually is a salesperson working under a broker. When you work with a fee-for-service agent, you are probably working directly with the broker.

Many fee-for-service agents are brokers who have given up the hassle, stress, and competition of a large office to go back to working for themselves. And one of the easiest ways to get started, particularly if they have an initial cash flow problem, is fee-for-service. This can be both good and bad for you. It is good in the sense that usually a broker has a higher level of experience, if not expertise, than a salesperson. It is bad in that it might indicate this broker had a lot of trouble making a go of it in real estate.

• *Can you give me references?* Any good agent can do this. And most are happy to do so. In the case of a fee-for-service agent, it should be particularly easy since this person, presumably, has more clients, albeit for smaller amounts.

Try to get a half dozen references and then call several of them. Ask them what type of service they paid for and whether they were satisfied with it. You should be able to tell pretty quickly if this agent has a long list of satisfied clients.

To do a thorough job, you'll also want to check with your state's division of real estate for any complaints against the agent. And, as with checking up on any business, you could also check for any complaints filed with your local Better Business Bureau and district attorney's office.

What if There Is a Problem?

This can happen with any agent. However, if you're paying for a specific service, the problem is more likely to be specialized. You may have paid to have your property listed on the MLS and it's still not on the service. Or, perhaps you're paying to have the agent answer calls on your ad and learn that people who call only reach an answering machine. Or you've found a buyer and you want to have the agent draw up the purchase agreement, but you can't get hold of the agent and time is slipping away.

If you have a problem, first try to contact the agent to see if it can be corrected. Often, it's simply a misunderstanding or lack of communication. Or maybe the agent just plain forgot and a little nudging will help.

It is more troublesome when you can't find the agent. Most people in business keep normal business hours. If your agent is away from the office a lot and can't be reached, it's probably a good reason to take your business elsewhere. Every business-person today can carry a cell phone and should be reachable within a few minutes.

The most difficult problems occur when your agent has provided a service for you that has gone sour, such as a purchase agreement that was filled out incorrectly or a contingent sale that has unraveled. Suddenly, you can't close escrow, or the buyer is screaming at you that your house can't pass inspection, or the lender refuses to fund the buyer, or . . .

When things go wrong, having a great agent makes all the difference in the world. If it turns out that the agent you have isn't so great, what are your alternatives?

Steps to Take When Problems Arise with a Fee-for-Service Agent

- Give your agent a chance to explain and, perhaps, correct the problem.
- Ask your escrow officer if he or she can help (often they are constrained by their position from doing so).
- Call in another agent to see if he or she can make things right.
- Check with your attorney to see if you have liability or should take any further action.
- Talk to your local real estate board.
- Talk to your state department of real estate.

12

Selling on Your Own

In the trade it's called FSBO (For Sale by Owner).
You've undoubtedly seen signs on homes for sale by owner. You can often tell because the "For Sale" signs tend to be amateur efforts, either made at home or bought at a local drugstore.

What they all mean is that no agent is involved. The seller is attempting to sell the home directly to the buyer with no middleman, which is obviously a hard sell. The seller is performing the work of the agent. If the seller is a purist (doing it without any professional help) that includes everything from promoting the property and finding a buyer to handling all the paperwork and closing escrow—a daunting task.

Why would a seller go through all that effort? The answer is, to avoid paying a commission. The following list shows what the seller would save, assuming a 6 percent commission, on houses at various price points:

Savings on a 6 Percent Commission

Sales Price	Savings
$ 150,000	$ 9,000
250,000	15,000
350,000	21,000
450,000	27,000
550,000	33,000
650,000	39,000
750,000	45,000
850,000	51,000
950,000	57,000
1,050,000	63,000

As you can see, the savings add up to serious money. On a half-million-dollar home (not an uncommon price in many areas today), the sellers can save over $30,000 by selling entirely on their own. That's quite an incentive. It is the price of a small luxury car. It can be a substantial portion of a year's worth of income. It represents one whale of a vacation.

It is easy to see why so many sellers are tempted to sell on their own. (Statistics suggest that between 10 and 15 percent of all home sellers do, in fact, sell on their own.) The real question is, can *you* do it? And, *should* you do it?

What It Takes to Sell on Your Own
Experience

Have you bought and sold many properties, either with an agent or on your own, before? If you were a hands-on buyer/seller, you probably have a thorough understanding of what's involved in a real estate transaction because you have actually gone through the process several times. If instead you were passive for the most part, simply signing the papers as they were laid in front of you, you could be as new to a real estate transaction as if you had never participated in one. If you haven't completed any real estate deals or have gone through them passively, you should stay away from trying to do it yourself. This is not something you can easily learn the first time out, and you are likely to encounter many difficulties. Active participation in buying and selling at least three or four homes is probably the minimum requisite for attempting to do it without an agent.

Time

Selling your home need not be a full-time job. You can do it on weekends, in the evenings, and in your spare time, provided you can get someone to cover for you the rest of the time. By "the rest of the time," I mean when a potential buyer calls and you're not available. Buyers call at their convenience, not yours. Thus, you need to have access to your phone virtually 100 percent of the time. One way to do this, although it might mean receiving calls at an importune time, is to link any numbers (such as an advertisement or website) to a cell phone that you keep with you. Another, but less effective, method is to link the number to an answering machine. The problem is that a would-be buyer may simply hang up and not leave a callback number or message.

It is a huge mistake to think that you can sell a home on your own without investing considerable time on the project. You'll need to set up promotions, get the property ready (which you would do anyhow), answer calls, show the home, handle negotiations, and close the escrow. Those are time-consuming tasks. If you can handle the time demands, then you're closer to meeting the "by owner" challenge.

Personality

You don't need the personality of a TV game show host to sell your home. You don't even need to be particularly gregarious. But, you do need to be able to talk pleasantly with people, gain their confidence, and "close" or sell them. Most people can do this. If you're not sure about yourself, think back to the times that you've been a salesperson. Have you ever sold a car, a boat, a bike, or other item? Was it difficult? Have you ever sold anything for a living, even subscriptions to magazines as a kid? Were you successful?

In some ways, selling your own home is easier. You already thoroughly know the product. You can speak at length (something you have to watch out for!) about its strong points. And you know its weak points. In fact, you could be the perfect salesperson for your home.

On the other hand, you will need to invite strangers into your home. You'll need to call back people who come by. You'll need to conduct negotiations for a very pricey product. You'll need to soothe, calm, and lead buyers who are skittish. If any or all of that makes you feel uncomfortable, you might be better off not trying to sell your home on your own.

Security

Are you willing to ask strangers into your home? In today's world, this can be dangerous. Although you can minimize the risk by always having a friend or relative present, you could unwittingly admit a thief, or worse. If you can't handle the risk, don't sell on your own.

From the preceding information, you should be able to make at least a tentative judgment about selling on your own. If you want to make the attempt, keep in mind that it is not an irrevocable decision. Any time that you get discouraged, you can break away and list with an agent. (Indeed, agents are almost always delighted to help people selling on their own because they know that most owners will eventually give up . . . and the agents hope to get that listing.)

How to Do It

To sell your home on your own, you essentially have to duplicate the work that an agent does. (You didn't think you'd save all that money without doing any work, did you?) To find out what an agent does, review Chapter 3. For now, however, let's just deal with the highlights.

Get a Sign

Seems obvious, doesn't it. Yet, some people think they can sell a house without a sign. It's like trying to sell groceries behind a blank storefront or lemonade at an unmarked stand on the street. Selling without a sign is almost impossible.

Your sign identifies your home to all those who are looking to buy: neighbors, drive-bys, and people who have responded to your ad and want to view your house.

It is worth the extra bucks to get a nice sign. You can order one at a sign shop for around $100. It will look just like the signs that agents use except that instead of giving an agent's name, it will simply say, "By Owner."

A big decision is the phone number you will put on the sign. If you choose your house phone, consider who else will be using it. Kids? Relatives? Will it be needed for emergencies?

If not your home phone, what about your cell phone? Will you have it always on? Is it automatically connected to an answering service? Can you customize the answer to indicate that the caller has, indeed, reached the number for the home for sale?

Also, you need to think about what else you want to put on the sign. Is just "For Sale by Owner" enough? Everything you put on the sign is likely to get noticed, unless the lettering is too small. Descriptive phrases such as "custom house" or "4 bedrooms" can help. Words like "pool" and "spa" (assuming you have them), also will attract interest.

Create a Flyer and Post It

Write it up. Mention all the amenities in your house. Let people know the number of bedrooms and baths, that the carpeting is new, that you have a pool/spa, that the house was recently painted, that new double-pane windows have been installed, and so on. Then add a nice color picture of the house, the price, address (unless you have security concerns), and your phone number.

Finally, attach a small plastic or wooden box to the post holding up your sign and stock the box with some of the flyers. Potential buyers who come by and pick up a flyer can see what you have to offer and quickly determine if they want to pursue the property, or forget about it. Providing that basic information can save you countless calls from people who aren't really interested in your home and may net you a few precious calls from people who are.

Make some extra flyers and distribute them to friends and associates at work, and ask relatives to hand them out to their friends and associates. Tack some up at supermarket and drugstore bulletin boards. If your place of business or employment has a housing office or employee notice board, leave some there. Let your flyers give you as much exposure as possible. They are one of the cheapest, yet most effective, means of advertising.

Including a picture is very important—if you have a digital camera, getting the picture is a breeze. You may want to take several shots. Then, using a program such as Photoshop on your computer (or one of the many easy-to-use digital imaging programs), you can print the images right on the flyer. Alternatively, you can have a copy store such as Kinko's do it for you. If you don't have a digital camera, you can use a tiny film throwaway, get a bunch of shots printed, and paste one on each flyer.

Get a Website

If you have a computer and an Internet Service Provider (ISP), you can quickly set up a website for your house. AOL, Yahoo!

and other providers offer space for this. If you're not sufficiently computer literate to handle this, see if there isn't a youngster in the family (or neighborhood) who can do it for you. (Kids today grow up around computers the way most of us mature citizens grew up around cars.) And once your site is up, you can get it listed on several search engines.

A website allows you to provide a wealth of information about your home in a venue that is easily accessed. Today, most people have the ability and the computer to get to your site. Be sure to put lots of pictures on your website. Again, this is easy to accomplish using either a digital camera or scanned photos from a film camera.

Advertise

You need to alert potential buyers that you have a house for sale. A sign is important, but buyers who don't drive down your street won't see it. You have to reach a larger audience. And newspaper advertising is the best bet in most circumstances. You don't need a large ad. Three or four lines is usually adequate. Emphasize that your home is for sale by owner and list its most attractive attributes. (If you are in a good school district, near a popular shopping center, have easy access to freeways or have a large lot, lots of square footage, or some other desirable feature, be sure to include that information in the ad.)

Give your phone number, and be sure you have linked it to your cell phone or answering machine. And be prepared to receive calls.

Prepare a Spiel

It's important to understand that calls from potential buyers are not personal calls. The would-be buyers on the other end aren't interested in hearing about your day, your medical problems, or the weather. These callers have a specific purpose—to find out whether your house is worth seeing. Or, to put it another way, they're looking for reasons to eliminate your house from their list of possible properties. Thus, you have only a few moments to establish rapport and to get them interested in what you have to sell.

You need to put together a spiel, or sales pitch, that that concisely incorporates all the important features of your home. For example:

Buyer: Hi, are you the person who has the house for sale?

Seller: Yes, you've reached the right person. We have a large, well-located and very clean home for sale. May I tell you about it?

Buyer: Sure, but we're looking for a home in the Maple Elementary school district and your ad says your house is in that district, right?

Seller: Quite right. We're in Maple. Our own children went there and it's a wonderful school. There are great teachers and they encourage parents to participate in the classroom. You'll love it.

Buyer: Yes, we think so. Well, that's great, now about the house?

Seller: We have four bedrooms, all with new paint and carpeting. There are three bathrooms, two were recently remodeled with new tile and fixtures and fresh paint. The kitchen is large with room for a table and four chairs. The appliances were replaced about five years ago, so they work perfectly and look new. At that time, we also put in granite countertops and added recessed lighting.

We are on a large lot. However, it doesn't require lots of maintenance because we have a wide cement driveway and plenty of stonework.

We have a three-car garage and the home has lots of storage. It is a two-story colonial and has over 2,300 square feet.

Would you like to see it? I'd be happy to show it to you.

It all seems to tumble out effortlessly. However, the seller has previously written down all the essential information from the capacity of the garage to the new paint and bathroom fixtures. And the seller gets these facts across after rapidly establishing rapport (by pointing out that the home is, indeed, in the school district that the buyer wants).

Your home will have different positives, and you will establish rapport by focusing on each caller's specific priorities. Just as with public speaking, however, you have to practice your spiel if you want it to sound effortless. Write down every point you want and need to get across and keep a copy of your notes by your home phone as well as with your cell phone so that you don't forget and leave something out when you're talking with a caller.

Create a Call Referral Sheet

This is important because you need to remember who called in case you want to call the person back. You might have a wonderful conversation with someone who seemed very interested in your home. Half an hour later, you remember something important that you should have told the caller. But, you can't recall the party's name, phone number, or both. You need a call referral sheet. At some point in the conversation, ask for the caller's name and number. Then jot it down, and after ending the conversation, add a few notes about the points you discussed. Now you can call back. And you should if the person doesn't contact you again within a few days. Ask whether you can answer any more questions about your house. Strike up a conversation. You just might respark interest in your property.

Prepare a House Tour

You're the person who's going to show your home. So get ready for it. Sometimes it helps if you rehearse with a friend or relative.

After you open the door and welcome the potential buyers, ask them to sign your guest register, which you should have ready. Try to get them to give their address as well as their phone number. (It's usually easiest to get them to do this when they first arrive.)

Getting would-be buyers to sign in is important for two reasons. First, like the call referral sheet, the guest register is useful if you want to call visitors back to see if you can spark interest in buying your home.

Second, you can use the register to exclude people who come by. If you eventually decide to give an agent an exclusive right-to-sell listing (see Chapter 9), you can identify these people as your buyers. If they later turn up and want to purchase, you don't owe a commission because they saw your house through you *before* you listed. You should give a copy of your list of exclusions containing names, phone numbers and, if possible, addresses to your agent at the time you sign the listing.

After the buyers have signed the register, slowly walk them through your house. Try not to spend too much time in any room. You don't want them to get bored. But give them enough time to look around. Sometimes it's a good idea to end up outside in the backyard. You might want to leave them there for a few moments while you go back inside. This gives them a chance to think about the house and perhaps discuss it.

Finally, bring them back in and ask them if they like the place. Chances are they will be polite and say they certainly do. Then ask them if they are interested in buying it.

At this point, they'll probably say they want to think about it. A good way to begin negotiations is to assume that their answer means they have reservations about the property. Ask them what they don't like about your home and stress that you want them to be brutally honest.

When they tell you, *don't argue.* But instead, point out positives that can overcome their objections. In this way you can begin a dialogue that may eventually lead to their agreeing to purchase.

How to Handle a Sales Agreement

If someone wants to buy your home, you need to get it in writing. (The statute of frauds adopted by virtually all states specifies that agreements to purchase real estate MUST be in writing to be enforceable.) Therefore, you need a written purchase/sales agreement.

This is what the agents use to write up a deal. Unless you're a licensed agent or attorney (or incredibly knowledgeable and up-to-date on real estate law), do *not* try to draw this up yourself. Instead, have a fee-for-service agent (see Chapter 11) or an attorney prepare it for you. The few dollars it costs will be well spent and could help you avoid a lawsuit later on.

Determine Where to Open Escrow

Nearly all real estate transactions involve an escrow. This is a company that acts as a stakeholder, an independent third party that receives money, handles and prepares documents, and eventually records title in favor of the buyers (and the lender) and sends you a check.

Escrow companies abound and are often tied together with title insurance companies (buyers and lenders want title insurance to protect their interests). Ask a real estate agent to suggest a reliable one. Also check with friends, relatives, or associates who recently bought or sold property. They can often relate satisfactory experiences, or terrible ones, that can help guide your decision.

Just show up at the escrow company with your sales agreement and deposit. The officer will be able to quickly open an escrow. Keep in mind, however, that if for some reason the escrow never closes (your deal falls through), you could be responsible for at least a portion of the escrow fee (see Chapter 14 for suggestions on reducing escrow and title insurance charges).

Give Buyers the Necessary Disclosures

Most states as well as the federal government mandate specific disclosures that the seller must give to the buyer. Any good agent should be able to help you with these disclosures. Specific deadlines often are involved. For example, the federal lead disclosure gives the buyer at least 10 days after receiving it to withdraw from the deal if lead is found. State disclosures have other time limits. Thus, you want to take care of these requirements as early in the transaction as possible.

Deal with Inspection Reports

There undoubtedly will be several inspections. The buyers will almost always want to schedule their own professional inspection of the home. Lenders will demand a termite clearance, which involves getting a termite inspection and removing infestation (if any) and making repairs (as needed). There could be other inspections of the roof, soil, structure, and so on.

You need to know which are due when and keep on top of them. Typically, the buyers have 14 days to obtain and approve a professional home inspection, which they pay for. If they don't approve the findings, the deal could be off. You usually have until closing to obtain and pay for a termite clearance. However, since getting the clearance involves having an inspection and possibly doing repair work, you should take care of it early.

Again, check with an agent or real estate attorney if you're not sure what needs to be done and when.

Closing the Escrow

To close the escrow, the buyers usually remove all their contingencies (financing, inspection, disclosures, and so on); the lender funds the new loan; the buyers deposit the down payment into escrow; and a clear title is recorded. The process may not seem like a lot to handle when the major events are written down as they appear here, but they can involve a great many details. You need to check on the escrow daily to be sure things are being done properly and as needed. If you don't take care of it, no one else is likely to do it.

Eventually, things usually come together, the deal is ready to close, and everyone signs off. And then escrow closes.

Move!

If possible, don't move until escrow has closed and the title has been transferred. It is too easy for something to go wrong at the last minute. If you've already moved and the deal can't close, you might have to move back. What's worse, the buyers might have already moved in and they'll have to move out. It could turn into a nightmare.

Once escrow has closed and the deed has been recorded in favor of the buyers, it is no longer your home. It is time to move out. Usually you can do this in an orderly fashion by contacting the buyers and arranging for the date and time of transfer. Then you move, give them their keys, and get on with your life!

For more information on selling on your own home, check into my book, *The For Sale by Owner Kit* (Chicago: Dearborn, Fourth Edition, 2002).

 **13**

Determining the Worth of Your Home

The pricing of your home is crucial to its sale. If it's priced too high, buyers won't come by and the listing will get stale, sitting unsold on the market. If it's priced too low, you'll lose money.

Thus, even before negotiating the commission, you need to know what your home is worth.

Do Neighbors, Agents, or Appraisers Know?

One way to find out what your home is worth is to ask your neighbors. Most owners these days carefully watch the sales of homes in their neighborhood. Even If you aren't keeping track, your neighbors are aware of current prices in your area. They may know that the Greens, down the street, sold a home just like yours for $310,000 four months ago. And the Smiths up the street sold one similar to yours for $333,000 only a month ago. Thus, your neighbor may conclude that your home is worth the later, higher price of $333,000. How accurate or scientific is that? Most neighborhood pricing opinions are based on testimonials, which are often notoriously off base.

Or, you can ask your agent. Agents can provide more accurate information because they have access to a computerized system that will pop out a list of recent prices for similar homes sold in your area. Some of the computer programs will even generate a comparative market analysis (CMA) report. It will compare your home with those recently sold to come up with a price.

Can you rely on that price? Maybe, since it's based on comparable home sales.

Finally, you can hire an appraiser. Few people use this approach because appraisers generally charge in the $300 range and often do exactly what the agent does: They get a list of homes comparable to yours and from that deduce a price.

All these methods will get you to a price. But, in addition to at least asking neighbors and your agent, you also need to do your own investigation, particularly of the current market conditions.

Creating Your Own Pricing Report

Begin with a CMA, produced by an agent. But, then check it out very carefully. Typically, it is derived from MLS listings. It shows the listing price, the sales price, and all the features of comparable homes that have been recently sold—from square footage, to bedrooms and baths, to pools and spas.

My experience is that sometimes these CMAs are way off. Often they list homes with the same or similar square footage as yours in your neighborhood, and then use their selling prices as a basis for the value of your home.

There are two things wrong with this method. First, the sale price of another home is not the listing price. And since buyers often offer less than list, if you list at recent sales prices, you're going to get lots of lowball offers and, perhaps, lose money.

Second, the homes used as comps may not really be comparable. The exact same model home as yours (same square footage, bedrooms, and bathrooms) may actually be worth far more than your home if the owners remodeled the kitchen and baths with new fixtures, appliances, and granite countertops; installed expensive carpeting; repainted throughout; and put in new double-pane windows. Your home with the original tile kitchen and baths, old cabinets, old carpeting and paint, and old metal windows simply isn't going to command as high a price. Indeed, if you try to get what your neighbors got for their completely refurbished home, chances are you'll be sadly disappointed.

And what if the tables are turned? What if yours is the home that's been completely refurbished? And the comparable is the home that hasn't had any renovations?

An agent may press you to sell for a price close to the comparable's sales price. If you do that, your home will probably sell as soon as it goes on the market, because it will be a steal. Your home is going to be worth far more because of what you've done to it.

Note: This doesn't mean that you can always get back every penny you put into your house. You can over-renovate your home for the location it is in and lose money. Nevertheless, an upgraded house is definitely worth more than one that hasn't been improved.

Thus, you need to take a close look at the comps. And then you need to take a close look at your house. And, finally, you need to use common sense. Adjust the value of your house up or down, based on the condition of your property and the comparables.

Take Market Trends into Account

While looking at comps includes viewing the market in a general way (after all, we're talking about actual sales), it doesn't look closely at trends. I see this all the time with houses that either don't sell for months on end, or sell within days. The sellers may have checked the comps, but they didn't take market trends into consideration.

The housing market is volatile. It's almost always going up or down. It seldom remains static for long periods. That means the value of your home is going up or down all the time, too. Between the time the comps were sold, prices may have adjusted upward or downward. Your own home's price should reflect this change.

You should try to determine the market trends in your area, which is often more easily said than done. Many local newspapers print monthly, or even weekly, reports on the status of home sales by neighborhood or, more likely, by zip code. They may be up 2 percent (on an annualized basis) one month and down 3 percent the next. Usually, however, they will trend upward or downward.

There also are national services that report on housing trends. The website dataquick.com may send you a free monthly report on home sales price trends in your zip code area. (For $9.95 you can obtain a homes sales report on your house in your neighborhood.) Other major real estate websites offer similar services (check with a good search engine such as google.com and use keywords like "real estate appraisal," "home price," and "home valuation").

Plot the trends in your neighborhood. Here is a sample price chart for a common zip code. The prices are given monthly:

Typical Trend by Zip Code

Year	Month	Median Price
2003	1	$280,000
2003	2	279,000
2003	3	280,000
2003	4	282,000
2003	5	281,000
2003	6	280,000
2003	7	282,000

Year	Month	Median Price
2003	8	283,000
2003	9	284,000
2003	10	287,000
2003	11	293,000
2003	12	299,000

The preceding monthly figures show that in the first part of the year, prices were fairly stagnant hovering around the $280,000 mark. However, during the second half of the year, prices accelerated upward. During the past six months, prices moved up higher every month and accelerated rapidly during the last 3 months of the year.

If you are selling in January, what does this tell you? It tells you that comparables from the first half of the previous year are largely irrelevant. They represented a period of static sales, before prices began to move.

On the other hand, comparables taken from the second half of the year, especially those more than two or three months out, are going to be too low. Prices began to accelerate upward only in the last few months of the year.

If we were to project prices for January and February based on the preceding chart, they might look something like this:

Typical Trend by Zip Code

Year	Month	Median Price
2004	1	$305,000
2004	2	311,000

This presumes that recent trends will continue. Thus, if you were to look at a CMA based on the previous six months, it might show that the average price of homes sold in your area was around $290,000. However, if you then planned on selling your home for $290,000 in February of the next year, you could be missing the market by $21,000. Your asking price would be too low, and you would lose money.

This is why you should use a CMA with caution. Yes, it's helpful. But, always use an additional tool that shows market trends. Although in our example, prices were trending upward, they could just as easily be trending downward. The prices in February could have been lower than those in February of the previous year, which happens in a buyer's market.

Trends can easily fool us by pretending to be self-perpetuating. If prices are increasing by $5,000 a month, we've established a trend. So projecting into the future, it may seem reasonable to assume that next month's prices will likewise be $5,000 higher, but that pattern is not inevitable. Trends are based on supply and demand—the number of buyers out there as well as the number of houses for sale. And they are also based on the economic health of the country and your local area. Beware of basing your judgment completely on trends. The trend could turn around the very month you're projecting.

Consider Economic Conditions

Over the long term, the health of the economy both nationally and locally, can make a big difference in how trends develop, peter out, and change direction. Be particularly concerned about jobs and interest rates.

People buy homes when they have jobs and feel secure about keeping those jobs in the future. If jobs are scarce and people are increasingly being laid off, buyers feel insecure and may be unwilling to risk making a huge investment in a house.

Therefore, check the job picture in your area. But keep in mind that like politics, jobs are all local. This is why housing sales and prices dipped in Michigan and Silicon Valley, California, in the early 2000s, while they were rising in New York and Boston. The job market was falling in Silicon Valley, but it was booming elsewhere. Where do you think people felt confident and secure enough to buy? Where did they worry and stay away?

When jobs are scarce, wages tend to remain stagnant. When that happens even those who have jobs often are unable to purchase homes at high prices because their income is inadequate. Thus, a poor job market rubs two ways against housing. On the other hand, when the job market is busy and there are plentiful jobs and increasing wages, the effect on housing is doubly positive.

Finally, there's the matter of interest rates. The housing market is interest rate sensitive. When rates are low, more houses will sell than when rates are high.

This only stands to reason since mortgage payments are based on the interest rate. If the maximum you can afford each month, given your income, is $1,500, then at 5 percent interest, you can afford about a $280,000 mortgage. But, if interest rates rise to 7 percent (and the maximum monthly payment you can afford remains at $1,500), then the maximum mortgage you can afford drops to $225,000.

The 2 percent rise in interest rates has cut your maximum mortgage by $55,000. And, since most buyers rely on big mortgages to purchase property, your ability to pay for a home has likewise been dramatically cut.

This is why there is a dramatic increase in home sales when interest rates fall. The additional buyers who can purchase more expensive homes drive the market to increase home prices.

Similarly, when interest rates increase, fewer buyers can get big mortgage or afford high-price homes. Hence, they are forced to buy less expensive properties. And as the market is forced to reevaluate, prices begin to drift down in search of buyers.

The National Association of Realtors (NAR, Realtor.org), provides an affordability index both nationally and by region of the country. It indicates on a constantly changing basis how well the median family (based on income) can afford a median-price home. You can check this index to see how your area of the country is faring. Keep in mind that when fewer and fewer people can afford housing, the number of sales and eventually prices, will trend down. And when more and more people can afford homes, the sales and prices will trend in the other direction.

There is a peculiar phenomenon about interest rates that needs to be mentioned. Generally, their effect on housing tends to be directed more to the lower end of the market.

This means that the lower your home is priced, the more sensitive it will be to interest rate trends. Likewise, the higher your home is priced, the less sensitive it will be. Thus, someone selling a $100,000 home should do much better in a low interest rate environment than in a higher rate period. Someone selling a million-dollar house is less likely to be affected by interest rates.

The reasoning here appears to be that people who buy less expensive homes need a big mortgage to make the purchase. People who can afford million-dollar homes often have much more available cash to put into the property and hence are less affected by interest rates.

Small interest rate movements tend to move the market very little. If interest rates drop from 6 to 5 percent or rise from 5 to 6 percent, there probably will be very little change in the number of sales or the effect on pricing.

When interest rates move by more than 2 percent, however, the change tends to be more obvious. If rates move from 7 to 5 percent, you might expect to see a big surge in volume and prices. Similarly an increase from 5 to 7 percent could herald a slowdown in volume and at least a slight reduction in prices.

Finally, when the market goes bad, the volume of sales usually drops quickly. But prices tend to drop slowly. When the market gets better, the volume of sales goes up slowly, but the prices tend to rise quickly.

14

Reducing Your Closing Costs

It's great to save money on the commission when you sell your home. But, why limit yourself? If you're careful, you may also be able to save money on your closing costs.

Closing costs would be better named *transaction costs*. They are the price of all the other things that are necessary to sell your home. For a seller, the following items are typical closing costs:

- Commission
- Title insurance
- Escrow fee
- Attorney fee
- Termite clearance
- Repairs as demanded by buyer

Closing costs for the seller, exclusive of commission, which has already been discussed in detail, can range from 1 to 4 percent of the selling price of a home. If your home sells for $200,000, it would not be uncommon for you as the seller to have between $2,000 and $8,000 in closing costs. As the price of your home goes up, so do the closing costs.

That is serious money. Reducing those costs, therefore, is a serious matter.

Hardballing the Buyer

In a seller's market, it is sometimes possible to reduce or eliminate closing costs entirely. Sellers have been using this technique in today's tight housing market. With home prices high and inventory low, sellers have been in a strong negotiating position and can often dictate terms. For most sellers, this has meant pushing for a higher price. For other savvy sellers, however, this has also included demanding that buyers pay some or all of the seller's closing costs. Here's how it works.

In a typical real estate transaction, buyer and seller both have closing costs, but depending on the negotiations, either party can pick up part or all of the other's closing costs. In a tight market where plenty of buyers are competing for relatively few homes, some sellers have demanded, and have gotten, buyers to pay their costs.

For the buyer, it's another item in the cost of the home (albeit it's a *cash* item). Since most buyers have trouble coming up with additional cash, they often resist paying the seller's costs, but they may acquiesce if it's the only way to get a home they want. For the seller, the arrangement simply means more take-home.

The actual method of handling the transaction is straightforward. As part of the negotiations, the sellers make it a contingency in a "subject to" clause that is written right into the purchase agreement. Unless the buyers agree to pay the sellers' closing costs, the sale's off.

Yes, this could lose a sale. But some sellers are willing to take the risk in a strong market. In a normal-to-weak market, this ploy rarely works. Many buyers simply refuse to pay the sellers' closing costs and walk away from the purchase. Thus, you must use this tactic judiciously.

Cutting Individual Costs

In this section, we consider each of the various elements in the closing costs.

Title Insurance

This insurance protects the buyer against problems with the title to your property. Unlike most insurance, which protects against future happenings, title insurance protects against past occurrences. It protects the buyers of your property against a defective deed caused by such things as a forged signature, improperly drawn documents, and sometimes even inaccurate boundary lines.

While it would seem logical that the buyers would pay for this insurance, since they're the ones being protected, who pays for it is largely a matter of local custom. In some areas, the buyers foot the bill. In other areas, it's the sellers. And in some locales, the buyers and sellers split the cost.

If you're responsible for paying the title insurance bill, see if you can select a title insurance company that charges less. This may not be possible for two reasons. First, it may be illegal for you to demand your choice of title insurance company, according to Real Estate Settlement Procedures Act (RESPA). You may be limited to making suggestions.

Second, in some states, title insurance fees are set by the state. In most states, however, they are determined competitively.

Another method of getting the amount reduced may be possible if you've recently purchased the home you're selling and have the right to select the title insurance company. If you bought your home within the past three years or so, you can ask the original title insurance company (the one that handled your purchase) to give you a "reissue" fee. This fee is reduced, sometimes by as much as half, because the company is essentially reissuing the same title policy to new owners. It is certainly worth checking out.

———

Note: Sometimes lenders will demand a more extensive policy of title insurance called an American Land Title Association (ALTA).

Since this is a demand of the buyer's lender, the buyer should foot the bill. However, as noted, local custom often determines who covers this expense.

Escrow Fee

The escrow is a neutral third party that holds all documents and money. The escrow is "perfect" when all the contingencies have been removed, the monies are all in place, and you've signed the deed. Then the escrow records the deed in favor of the buyers and issues you a check.

Typically, licensed corporations run escrow companies, sometimes in conjunction with title insurance companies. Their fees can vary widely. In recent years, rising home prices have led a few escrow companies to charge outrageous fees. Sometimes the fees at one escrow company are double or even triple the fees at another one. If you are going to be paying all or part of the escrow fees, it will be well worth your time to check out several companies to determine which firm charges the least. (If you're splitting the cost with the buyers, let them know the problem. Once they understand, they will probably support you in your efforts to reduce expensive escrow fees.)

Also, be sure to ask about the total costs. Some escrow companies have a single all-inclusive fee. Others have a basic fee and then charge for a lot of minor services. Sometimes the company with the lowest basic fee can end up having the highest total cost once you have tallied all the additional services.

Finally, sometimes attorneys will run escrows, particularly on the East Coast. If they do, they often will lump the cost in with an overall charge for handling the legal aspects of the transaction for you. Typically this cost is under $1,500, usually a real bargain.

Attorney Fee

As noted, you may use an attorney to handle parts of the closing for you. Although these fees are usually reasonable, you should check them out in advance. Some attorneys charge by the hour and others by the service performed. Usually, but not always, the latter results in a lower total overall cost.

Be wary of being charged for attorneys who do not work for you. Sometimes other parties to the deal will want you to pay for their attorney's work. This can include the title insurance company, the escrow company, and/or the lender. The general rule I follow is, if I didn't hire the attorney, I shouldn't have to pay that attorney's bill.

Termite Clearance

Almost always, the sellers will be asked to provide a termite clearance for the house. This is a document that says that the home is free from termites and certain other kinds of infestation. Getting this clearance can be difficult. Normally, only a licensed termite inspector can issue it and will do so only after thoroughly inspecting your property. Thus, you'll have to pay for a termite inspection, which usually costs a few hundred dollars.

Depending on your locale and house, the inspector may very well find termites. If so, then you'll usually have to pay for an extermination and repair any damage. This can get expensive.

Whereas the cost of a termite inspection tends to be fairly standard across most companies, the costs of removal and repair can vary dramatically. If the inspector quotes an exorbitant amount to get that clearance, get a second opinion from another company. Most termite inspection companies are ethical, but there's an inherent conflict of interest if the inspector is also the one who does the removal and repair. Sometimes, the best way to remove the termites and make the repairs is a matter of opinion, even among experts. And one opinion could be considerably cheaper than another.

Remember, your goal is to get the piece of paper that clears your property. It usually doesn't matter which licensed inspector issues it or how the work was done.

Repairs Demanded by Buyers

This also can be an expensive area. Today, buyers undoubtedly will want a professional inspection of the home as part of their purchase decision. (The sale will be contingent on the buyers approving an inspection report.)

Unless your house is relatively new, chances are that the buyers will find something on the report that they will not approve. Usually the most expensive items are either a leaky roof or structural damage. However, the report can note things as simple as a leaky faucet or a leaning fence.

When buyers disapprove an inspection report, they will then usually present you, the seller, with a list of demands. They will buy the property *only* if you correct the defects they have noted. Sometimes there's a long list of minor items. You might be able to fix faucets, repair screens, and replace lightbulbs on a weekend.

On the other hand, the list may include some very costly items. The buyers may want you to put a new roof on the house.

Or they may want you to jack up the house and pour a new foundation. Or they may want you to restucco the entire exterior.

Again we're back to serious money. Here are four suggestions for minimizing the cost of these repairs:

1. *Refuse to do them.* Sometimes if you refuse, the buyers will withdraw their demands and proceed with the purchase, absorbing the costs themselves. This happens more often in a hot market. Your risk, however, is that the buyers will back out of the deal, usually without losing their deposit, and you will lose the sale.

2. *Do them yourself.* I don't mean physically do them yourself. I mean that if you agree to the repairs, then you can hire the contractor who is going to deal with them. That way you can control the costs. If the buyers hire the contractor, and you're paying for it, they're very likely to get the most expensive one out there. Or, alternatively, if the job isn't too big and you're capable, you may want to do it yourself and save a bundle.

3. *Offer a money settlement.* Here, instead of making the repairs, you offer a compromise between buyer and seller. If it will cost $15,000 to restucco the exterior of the home, you acknowledge that the existing stucco has a lot of cracks and that the work needs to be done. But, you point out that you've only lived in the home for 7 years and it's 27 years old. Further, the buyers will get the benefit of the new stucco exterior for all the years they live in the house. Why, therefore, should you have to foot the entire bill? You offer to pay half, or $7,500. Once again, if it's a tight market, there are few homes, and the buyers really

want your place, they may agree. Or, they could walk and you could lose the deal.

Note: Be careful here—sometimes the buyer's lender will refuse to issue a new loan until the repair work is completed.

---

4. *Get your own report.* Just because the buyer's inspector says that you need a new roof or new plumbing or a new drainage system, doesn't make it so. Get your own report. Preferably, hire a specialist (as opposed to the generalist that the buyers usually hire). I recently sold a home that, according to the buyer's inspector, required an extensive drainage system for the front yard including a sump pump to keep rainwater runoff away from the house. I hired a soil specialist who determined that the problem was caused not by rainwater per se, but by clogged gutters and drains. For a fraction of the cost that the buyer's inspector and contractor had estimated, I had the drains and gutters cleaned and provided a pipe runoff system. This repair solved the problem, and I saved my money. Sometimes getting your own expert can make all the difference.

By being inventive and determined, you often can save lots of money on repairs when you sell your home.

Miscellaneous Costs

Many other costs can crop up when you're trying to close a home sale. They run the gamut from document preparation fees to courier charges to second escrows. (Sometimes a lender or a buyer/seller will need a second escrow linked to the first for handling a mortgage or other home sale.)

Question all such charges. Find out if they are legitimate (they actually were incurred and you are being billed the actual amount, not a higher amount with a tacked-on fee). Find out if they were supposed to be charged to the buyers or even the agents. Try to negotiate a lower amount. (Charges in a gray area probably can be reduced if you complain long and loud enough.)

Appendix A

Adding Value: Fixing Up Your House

You can spend hours negotiating the commission rate with an agent, but it will all be wasted time if your house doesn't look presentable. It is better to pay full commission and fix up your property than to get a cut rate but offer a distressed home to buyers.

If you want to sell, your property needs to have the charm of a dollhouse. Agents can give many hints on how to do this. Usually they'll tell you to mow the lawn (see Appendix B) and repaint a bit. Here are some less common suggestions that I've found particularly helpful.

Begin with the front. Some homes have a particular architectural style—Cape Cod, Southern Plantation, Spanish, Midwestern barn, or whatever. What style is your home?

If you answer that it's California Ranch, then ask yourself, "How well does it fulfill that style?" Does the house have vertical wood paneling, low brick or stonework, and a covered front patio? Or is there just a suggestion of these? Perhaps you can do more to make it look better within its style.

Or your answer may be that your home exhibits no particular style. It is just a box like many other homes built over the past few years.

Now, ask yourself if you're happy with the style and appearance of your home. This is more than just asking if the paint looks good or if the front door needs to be replaced. I'm asking, does your home have character?

Character is good, but out of character is bad. No matter what, you don't want your home to look abnormal for the neighborhood. You can do lots of things to stylize your house, but be careful not to overdo the decor. Creating an Oxford cottage in an area of angular modern homes will make it a fish out of water. You won't enhance the value of your property by making it unusual for its neighborhood. In fact, you could lower its value.

It is just as impossible to turn a Spanish bungalow into a, well, a New York brownstone as it is to turn a frog into a fawn. And it is foolish to attempt it. Except in unusual cases, increasing the value of your property by fixing up your home means *enhancing* its original style, not changing it.

Nowhere is this more evident than in San Francisco. Here, many of the homes were built around the end of the nineteenth century and had a Victorian façade. Hand-turned dowels gave a lacelike look to corners, and elaborate woodwork was the rule. Today, owners of these homes have spent substantial amounts of time and money to recreate the original Victorian look. (It's expensive, because when the houses were built, factories on the East Coast fabricated the necessary wooden parts and shipped them to California—today those factories are gone and the woodwork has to be reconstructed by hand.) However, owners usually get back all their money and more.

Many of today's renovations involve tearing down cheap siding and other alterations made to properties in the 1960s and 1970s. These changes contributed to keeping their price down. Some renovators, in fact, search out old Victorian homes that had bad fixes, buy them cheaply, restore them, and resell for a profit. That's probably the best argument for investing in the right kind of makeover.

Tips for Fixing Up Your Home

- *Determine whether your home needs it.* You might think that the front of your house looks fine. Or you might feel that it desperately needs a makeover. Either way, get second and third opinions. Talk to experienced real estate agents. Check with local architects. Speak to a home owner's association, if you have one. Consult with neighbors. Having other eyes look at your property is very helpful in coming up with ideas.

- *Do the cheapest repairs first.* Sometimes simply removing some old trellises or adding molding around windows is enough, and it can cost virtually nothing. Why spend big bucks when a cheap makeover will do?
- *Take a hard look at your windows.* Front windows often help style a home. You may be able to add a French window style, if appropriate, by replacing your existing windows with inexpensive retrofits. It can give your home a whole new look.

A simple fix-up that involves just changing the front accents might cost only a few hundred dollars and could return thousands. Do only whatever will enhance the appeal of your property, make the least expensive improvements first, and you should come out okay.

Replace or Clean the Carpeting

When potential buyers first enter a home, they glance all around the house. They look at chandeliers, room separators, wall coverings, the amount and type of furnishings—everything to get an overall sense of the place. Then, as they begin walking through your home, they look down to be sure of their footing so that they don't trip over something unexpected. And automatically, they focus on one of their most critical observations—your floors and floor coverings.

This evaluation continues as they walk through your home. People spend a lot of time looking down. And the condition of any carpeting on your floors is a huge factor in their assessment of both the quality and the condition of your home.

Attractive carpeting says this is a quality home, perhaps worth the price you're asking. Dirty, worn carpeting says that the buyers will have to spend big bucks to replace it, and no way will they give you your price. If a home has wall-to-wall carpeting, any real estate agent will advise the sellers to have it thoroughly cleaned before putting the home on the market. A soiled carpet looks terrible and distracts buyers from all the good features of a home.

If your wall-to-wall carpet is more than a few years old, cleaning may not be enough. All but the best-quality carpeting begins to show wear after it has been down just a few months, particularly in heavily trafficked areas. There will be matting and discoloration, with subtle changes in lift, color tone, and texture.

If your existing wall-to-wall carpet isn't spotless, perky, and generally looking great, the real answer is to replace it.

At this point, many readers who have had experience replacing carpeting probably are shaking their heads. Recarpeting a 2,000-square-foot home can easily cost $10,000 or more. Am I truly suggesting that someone do this to improve the value of the home for resale?

Indeed I am. Recarpeting is expensive, but if it is done correctly, the cost is also easily recaptured (and more) by a quicker sale and a heftier price. If your carpeting is worn to the point where it detracts from the appearance of your home, you're far better off dumping it and getting new.

Almost any quality of new carpeting will look better, at least for 6 months, than existing carpeting that is more than a couple years old. Builders of new homes realize this and frequently will install very inexpensive carpeting knowing full well that at least in the short haul, it will look great. And if you're contemplating selling soon, the short haul is your primary concern.

Further, it is almost impossible to really clean carpeting. It is not as if you can take it up and put it into the washing machine. Instead, it is a matter of inserting chemicals, steam, or water and extracting dirt. This process is far less than 100 percent efficient and sometimes leaves the carpeting stiff and ragged looking. After a few cleanings, the carpet will simply look worn out.

Inexpensive carpeting is available in most areas. For around $3,000 or less, you can carpet a 2,000-square-foot home with nylon carpeting that will initially look great. Spending three or four thousand dollars to put in new carpeting just before you sell is a no-brainer. It is an improvement that will sell your home fast and for more money.

You may not have carpeting at all. You might have wood flooring. All wood flooring, no matter the type of wood—even hard oak—will scratch over time. The more wear and tear on it, the worse it will look. If it's been three or more years since the wood flooring was last finished, it probably needs a new refinishing.

To properly refinish wood floors, the finisher must sand off the old finish and a thin layer of wood and then apply a new layer of sealant and some sort of stain or synthetic finish. This is a messy process. Because sanding raises so much sawdust, you usually must remove all your furniture from the house and store it elsewhere (not just in a different room, as with recarpeting) for a few days—sometimes for as long as a week. Also, the odor from the finishing products can be strong and may linger for several weeks.

The result, however, is usually spectacular. Your floors will shine and say, "Buy me!" to any potential buyers. And generally the cost is not as much as for new carpeting, depending on the condition of the floor and the type of wood.

Be leery of finishers who say they can strip the floors chemically. Though far cheaper than sanding, this method may not produce comparable results.

Paint Everywhere

Unless your home is almost brand-new, or you have just recently had it painted, you should seriously consider repainting the entire interior. Painting perks up a home and makes it look lively inside. It gives it a fresh, clean appearance that's attractive to home buyers.

You may be thinking to yourself, it'll cost a few thousand dollars to paint my house and I won't be putting it on the market for at least a year. Besides, it looks good. The current paint isn't bad.

If it will be awhile before you sell your home, then you can consider holding off on painting. Keep in mind, however, that the typically home needs to be repainted every five to seven years. Even if you plan to keep the house for some time, it may be time for a new paint job.

Don't ask yourself whether the paint looks good. Ask someone else. Bring someone in who hasn't gone through your house before (a real estate agent is a perfect candidate) and ask that person how the paint looks. An objective viewer will see scratches and marks that you have become blind to as well as dirt and faded colors that you've gotten used to. An honest answer may surprise you and convince you to repaint.

What about cleaning the walls instead? Don't do it. Unless you're talking about a very small area and then only in the kitchen or bath where high-gloss paints are typically used, don't even consider trying to clean the existing paint. It simply can't be done.

If the paint is more than a year old, it has a coating of dirt on it. You may not be able to see it. But dampen a sponge with a good cleaning agent, find a spot that's hidden, say in a closet, and run the sponge across the wall. The swipe immediately will stand out from the rest of the wall. There will be a color difference. Where you went across the wall, it is clean, the rest is dirty.

You may conclude from this that your walls need to be cleaned, and indeed they may need to be, before painting. However, unless you plan to go over every inch of wall and ceiling with a cleaner, probably several times, you won't get an even look. There will always be some areas that are cleaner and some dirtier. Trying to clean walls can become a career. It's much easier to paint. Clean off very dirty walls, and then paint over them. If you do it yourself, a roller and tray can make simple work of a wall. If you hire it out, you can probably get your entire house painted for around $2,500.

Beware of crayon and similar marks from grease pens. These will tend to bleed right through new paint. You can paint them a dozen times, and the marks will still show. The answer is to first scrape as much of the grease mark off as possible, and then use a shellac spray over it before painting. This seals the grease and allows the paint to cover and hide it.

In terms of color, the quick answer is to say just use light colors. White, in fact, is currently the most popular interior color. Most people, if nothing else, find light colors neutral and unobjectionable. That, however, begs the issue. Many upscale homes use a variety of harmonious colors including grays, reds, blues, and other deep colors that most of us would never consider using. I've seen homes with gray walls and orange ceilings that were incredibly beautiful.

It takes someone with real knowledge of color to be able to say what will and what won't work in a room. Therefore, before beginning to paint, go down to your local paint store and find out if they have a color consultant. Many paint stores, especially those that sell quality paints such as Benjamin Moore or Dunn Edwards offer color-matching services. For a small fee (or sometimes for free, if you agree to buy the paint), someone with a good sense of color will come out to your home with a color chart and make suggestions. (Alternatively, you can often hire a good interior designer to give you similar advice.)

Consider the various options you are shown. Sometimes color schemes that you never dreamed of will look terrific in your home.

Another approach finding considerable interest, particularly in children's rooms, is to stencil a border around the top, center, or bottom of a wall. The template used can feature almost any design from flowers to animals. Used sparingly, borders can add charm to almost any room.

Kitchens and baths are special cases. In bathrooms, use a high-gloss enamel paint that contains an antifungal agent. This will help keep mold from growing in this naturally damp area.

Be aware, however, that the best antifungal paint is typically oil-based, which means it smells bad and is tough to clean up. You may want to consider an exterior paint for your bathroom, which comes with strong antifungal agents.

For kitchens, a high-gloss paint is usually preferable because, unlike the flat paint used elsewhere in the house, it is easily cleaned. Again, an oil-based paint (as opposed to latex) usually works best here.

A special word if you're going to paint your cabinets. They may require special cleaning, sanding, and removal of old paint and stains. Before attempting to paint kitchen or bathroom cabinets, call in a professional painter for an expert opinion on how to do it, or even whether it can be successfully done at all.

Appendix B

Adding Value: Working on Landscaping

Landscaping dresses up your house, gives it appeal, and imparts a sense of quality. Good landscaping can add thousands of dollars to your home's value. And it makes your home easier and quicker to sell.

Yes, you can save thousands on the commission when you sell. But make thousands more by offering a well-landscaped house that will move fast at a better price.

Spruce Up the Front Lawn

Your front lawn is what potential buyers usually see first. Typically, it takes up the most space in front of the home. Therefore, your lawn should look terrific.

Of course, not all homes have a lawn. Many people use rock gardens, flowers, and bushes. These alternatives are fine, as long as they reflect the character of the neighborhood. If your house, however, is the only one without a lawn, a rock garden is going to look out of place even if it's gorgeous.

Get an experienced gardener or landscaper to appraise your lawn. If it looks mostly green, with a few yellow patches, that will be generally acceptable, but for a quick sale you want a lush full lawn that makes a potential buyer just want to roll around in it!

Usually, the problem with a patchy lawn is not enough water. Reseeding, aeration, and fertilization may do the trick if you can install an automatic watering system. But if your lawn still looks terrible, sometimes the best thing you can do is just replace it.

There are two ways to replace a lawn—sod or seed. Sod costs a hundred times more than seed, but you're almost guaranteed a great lawn. Seed can also produce great results, but only if you go through all the required steps: preparing the ground, seeding, watering, fertilizing, and so forth. In either case, you must first kill off and remove any old grass. A new average-size sod lawn can cost $1,500 or more. The cost of seed is only about $50.

Whether you put in a lawn from sod or from seed, it will only grow well if you water it deeply on a regular basis. Skimp on watering and you might as well forget about improving the value of your home through a new lawn. If you're retired (or work at home) and can afford to spend an hour or so a day watering your lawn with a hose, then you'll be fine. But if you're like most of us, you don't have the time to do that and, therefore, must invest in an automatic watering system.

Any underground sprinkler system should be installed *before* you put in your new lawn. You may simply want to have a landscaper put in the watering system and the lawn. It is the easiest, though the most expensive, way to go. Count on spending several thousand dollars for a good system. Or, you can do it yourself. The hard work is digging trenches. Almost anyone can glue together PVC pipe.

You can get plans for installing your own automatic sprinkler system at the store where you buy your sprinkler supplies or from the many books available on the subject. Just keep in mind that a good rule of thumb is to think in terms of more instead of less. More sprinklers and more watering stations usually mean a better lawn.

Note: Most communities require you to obtain a building permit before putting in a lawn sprinkler system. The reason is to ensure that you use "antisiphon" valves to avoid polluting your home's potable water system. It is a wise precaution, and you will want to be careful to follow all health and safety procedures.

A final word of advice: Be sure to install an automatic device to control your sprinklers, the kind you can set and forget. You can program which days to water, which stations to water, how long to water each station, and when to skip days. Then, these automatic devices just continue watering away on their own. The cost for the full system is usually not more than a couple hundred dollars.

One of the first steps in improving the value of your home is giving it better curb appeal. And the quickest way to improve that curb appeal is to transform a withered, dying, and yellowed old lawn into green, lush, and healthy grass. Put in a watering system (if you don't already have one), plant sod or seed, and enhance your home's value.

Note: Some people are absolutely obsessive about weeds in their lawn. They spend weekends poisoning and digging out weeds and then replanting grass. That much effort is unnecessary. First impressions do count, but they also tend to be superficial. A person driving up to your home likely will notice whether the lawn is patchy and brown, or solid green and well-mowed. But that person is unlikely to get down and check whether there are weeds in that green sea of grass. You need a good lawn. You don't need a perfect one.

Landscape Your Backyard

There are two ways to landscape a backyard. One way is to do it to please yourself. The other is to do it for effect—to please your potential buyers. Wise sellers think first about buyers, second about their own preferences.

Let's assume that you've done nothing to your backyard. It has weeds that are so tall you need a machete just to break trail and reach the back fence or end of your lot. Buyers who take a look at this will knock down the price of your home. They'll figure it will cost several thousand dollars to clean up the backyard and put it into shape.

Simply cutting down the weeds and cleaning up the yard will increase the value of your home. Rent a weed mower, and for about $50 you can add hundreds or more to your home's value. At least, you'll almost certainly get a quicker sale.

If you want to move a step up, then rent a rototiller and turn over the ground. Use a roller to flatten it and buy 50 bucks worth of seed. Spread it out, cover with a thin layer of soil amendment, and water the heck out of it. Two weeks later, you should have the beginnings of a lawn, and in a few months it should be thriving and green. Keep mowing and watering it, and soon it will become a lush, inviting expanse. For a hundred bucks or so, you've probably added a thousand or more to the value of your home (or at least kept it from being knocked down by that much).

From here, it gets harder. To keep a lawn going, you need a good watering system, as already discussed. That can cost anywhere from a few hundred bucks (if you do it yourself) to several thousand (if it is professionally installed). And you likely won't get any more for your efforts than if you simply drag a hose out and use a lawn sprayer.

You may also want to plant perennial flowers and shrubs around the periphery of the lot. These plants are inexpensive if you buy them when they are very small and cultivate them. After a year or so, they can develop into beautiful hedges, flower beds, and other decorative areas. Buyers who come by now will be even more impressed, will tend to make more offers, and may offer ever so slightly more. You probably haven't spent more than a few hundred dollars on flowers, so it's been worthwhile. Just remember that you'll be out there hand-watering every day or so unless you put in an automatic watering system (which is unlikely to increase the sales price of your house).

Finally, you can put in a patio deck. Decks are highly desirable in backyards. They give you a place to barbecue and to entertain guests, something that's definitely a plus. A deck can add $500 to $1,000 or more to the value of a home. However, you'll quickly find that decks can easily cost $5,000 or more to put in.

The typical deck is made either of wood or concrete. The concrete deck is the easiest to build. Simply level the soil, put down some gravel to even it out, cover with wire mesh or rebar to keep it from shifting, make a wooden form at the periphery, pour the concrete, and finish it. Today, however, concrete is expensive. So is wire mesh and rebar. And getting someone to pour and then to finish it is even more expensive. When done right, it looks impressive, but don't expect to recoup the full cost of putting it in.

Or, you can choose a wooden deck. These are typically raised a foot or so above the ground. They require footings, supports, joists, and wood decking that's resistant to mold, such as redwood or cedar. High-quality wood decking has become incredibly expensive. Installing a simple 10-by-15-foot wood deck (150 square feet) can easily cost $5,000.

Finally, consider the least expensive alternatives—bricks. These can be simple red bricks, paving stones, or almost any other kind of concrete or stone blocks. The smaller bricks are lighter and easier to handle. Assuming you have access, you can have them delivered right to where you want to build the deck. Then, you just level the ground, put down a bed of sand, and lay the bricks or stone. If you lay them side by side, you can fill the grooves with sand. Or, alternatively, you can plant grass between larger stones for a dramatic effect. (You can mow right over the stones.)

If you do it yourself, your only expense will be for the bricks or stones plus a little bit of sand and seed. Depending on the amount of material you need, the cost can easily be under $1,000. And the result can be a nice-looking patio deck that can boost the price of the home.

Consider the View from the Backyard

Unless you happen to have a dynamite view from your backyard, what most people want is privacy. They want to be able to go out into the backyard and have a picnic, to sit in the sun, to have the children play, and to do it all without having the neighbors looking in on them.

In some areas of the United States, primarily the Midwest and parts of the East, open spaces and no fences are the rule, making this is somewhat hard to achieve. But even so, taller trees and bushes, if appropriately placed, can curtain off at least a portion of the yard to give a strong sense of privacy.

Trees and tall bushes create a sense of spaciousness in a backyard in much the same way as tall ceilings expand a house. They force the viewer (the potential buyer) to look up and take in the three-dimensional area instead of just looking down at the lawn. A few strategically placed trees can make a small backyard seem to have vistas.

Then, there's the matter of shade. Well-placed trees can shade a house in the summer and reduce air-conditioning costs. And sitting in the shade of a beautiful oak or magnolia tree in the summer while sipping a light drink is one of life's nicer pleasures.

These factors—space, privacy, and shade—are going to influence what a buyer will be willing to pay. Although putting in elaborate landscaping is unlikely to get you a pumped-up price, putting in thoughtful landscaping to emphasize space and private areas can add to the home's value.

At the same time, beware of a fenced in look. Many people buy tall evergreens and plant them all along the periphery of the property. Instead of showing off spaciousness, such barriers visually shrink the dimensions of the yard. Tall trees can dwarf a deck and tiny plot of grass. They may increase privacy (in an overkill kind of way), but they work against spaciousness. You don't want to create the impression that you live in a little cottage in a giant, dark forest. You'll just scare buyers away. Instead, if you're going to plant taller trees, arrange them in clumps or groves. Three groupings is usually the maximum, one for each side of the backyard. And keep plenty of open space between them so that would-be buyers can see out as well as up.

If you hire a professional landscaper, you should have no problem here. Any competent landscaper or gardener will select trees and bushes that complement the size of the home and yard. If your home has a single level, you probably won't want any trees that are much more than 20 feet tall. That's a little above the height of a typical roof peak in a one-story home (usually 15 to 17 feet). If you have a flat roof, the trees should be around 10 or 12 feet tall, again to match the height of your roof. If you have a two-story, or even a three-story home, taller trees will work fine. Indeed, putting in shorter trees will only make the house look awkwardly disproportionate.

Choose the tall trees you plant with care. Pine trees are popular because they grow quickly; in a few years they can be 10 or 15 feet tall providing a pleasant appearance, shade, and privacy. Many varieties, however, grow to heights of 100 feet. True, it could take them 20 or more years to do so, but eventually they could tower over not only your house but also your entire neighborhood!

Fruit trees are a good choice for many backyards. Today, nurseries usually can tell you the maximum width and height the tree is likely to achieve. And many varieties of dwarf fruit trees are available. You can select the trees you want based on their ultimate size, the amount of shade they give, the color of the flowers they produce, and even the fruit they offer. Used sparingly, they provide an excellent way to inexpensively go tall in your backyard.

It may also be necessary to remove trees that are inappropriate for your backyard. Unless you have just moved into a brand-new home without landscaping, chances are you already have trees. And many of these, as noted, may be too tall or otherwise inappropriate. When that's the case, don't hesitate to remove them.

A word of caution: Hire a professional to take down tall trees. Felling a tree can be dangerous work. You may think it's simply a matter of buying a chain saw and making a couple of cuts, but if you cut wrong and that tree falls on you, or your neighbor's roof, you'll rue the day you decided to do it on your own. Reliable companies charge a lot—$500 to $1,000 per tall tree is not uncommon. But, then again, they have the knowledge to do it right, and they carry insurance to protect you if they make a mistake. (Any reputable tree service will show you a current policy of liability insurance for at least a million dollars or more.)

Note: Some cities and counties have restrictions on tree removal. They feel that trees contribute to the overall beauty of the community, and you need a permit to remove one, even if it is on your own property. If the tree is a protected species, you may not be able to take it down, even if you consider it an eyesore.

Beware: Do *not* harm a tree on your neighbor's property. In some states, the penalty is severe. In California, if you cut down your neighbor's tree without permission, you are liable for three times the cost of planting a new, similar tree!

What if You Already Have a Nice Backyard?

If your yard is nicely landscaped, then you simply need to clean, trim, and spruce it up. You may want to treat your patio deck with stain or sealant to sharpen its appearance. Wood can be pressure-cleaned with water and then stained. Bricks, stone, and cement can be chemically treated to get out most stains.

Backyards need to look neat, clean, and livable, but keep in mind that spending a lot of money on them is like digging a money pit.

Fix Those Fences

Given all the positives of fences, one would think buyers might consider them a necessity, but that's not always the case. In many parts of the country, most lots are unfenced. Because no strong dividers exist between neighbors' properties, there's much more open space and an atmosphere of living in a village. Sometimes fences isolate families.

Fences are a two-sided blade and can be beneficial as well as disadvantageous. One thing is certain, however; if you live in a neighborhood with fences, you must maintain your own. Letting a fence fall into disrepair makes the property look shoddy and distressed. Just repairing a fence and repainting or staining it can add thousands to the value of your home.

In tracts with a height restriction on fences, a living wall rising above that height can be considered just as much a violation as any other kind of fence, and a neighbor or a home owner's association could force you to cut it down. To avoid getting involved in a legal dispute over a fence or boundary (typically the nastiest kind of argument), check with the rules and bylaws of your home owner's association and the conditions, covenants, and restrictions (CC&Rs) in your neighborhood.

If you already have a fence in place and need to replace it, consider putting up one of like kind (wood for wood, stone for stone, cement block for cement block, etc.). There may even be a deed restriction on your property requiring a certain type of fence. Don't get carried away. Your fence needs to look good, but not elegant. If all the homes in the neighborhood have block wall fences, then that's what you should have. Putting up wood could cheapen your home. Putting in rocks could be overbuilding for the area.

Don't assume that the existing fence is on the property line. It might be; or it might not be. Get a survey to determine the correct boundary. Then, if it's entirely your fence, place it a few inches on your side. That way, your neighbor can't complain about it. If it's a "neighbor" fence, with each of you paying for half of it, you'll probably want to put it on the boundary line.

Fences can create a volatile situation. It may turn out that one of the main reasons your neighbors like their homes is that there is open space around them—a large part of which is on your property. When you fence it in, it could turn very nasty with neighbors even threatening lawsuits. First, as noted, be sure of your boundaries by getting a careful survey. Then, check to see if fences are allowed in your area. Check also with any home owner's association. Proceed only if you can meet all the legal requirements.

Some people advocate letting your neighbors know in advance. Others say, just do it and let it be a fait accompli. It really depends on your disposition and the kind of neighbors you have.

Finally, if you have never fenced a specific area and your neighbors and others have used it as a walkway for years, they may claim prescriptive rights to it as an easement. And you may have difficulty defending against that argument in court and legally putting up your fence.

Index